All I Ever Wanted
was to be Called

MOM

All I Ever Wanted was to be Called
MOM

*A Woman's Epic Quest for Salvation
on the Road to Motherhood*

VASPX
Steve and Vaso Petrou

New York

All I Ever Wanted was to be Called MOM

A Woman's Epic Quest for Salvation on the Road to Motherhood

Published in New York, New York, by Morgan James Publishing. Morgan James and The Entrepreneurial Publisher are trademarks of Morgan James, LLC. www.MorganJamesPublishing.com

The Morgan James Speakers Group can bring authors to your live event. For more information or to book an event visit The Morgan James Speakers Group at www.TheMorganJamesSpeakersGroup.com.

A free eBook edition is available with the purchase of this print book.

CLEARLY PRINT YOUR NAME ABOVE IN UPPER CASE

Instructions to claim your free eBook edition:
1. Download the BitLit app for Android or iOS
2. Write your name in **UPPER CASE** on the line
3. Use the BitLit app to submit a photo
4. Download your eBook to any device

ISBN 978-1-63047-665-6 paperback
ISBN 978-1-63047-666-3 eBook
Library of Congress Control Number:
2015908023

Cover Design by:
Rachel Lopez
www.r2cdesign.com

Interior Design by:
Bonnie Bushman
The Whole Caboodle Graphic Design

In an effort to support local communities and raise awareness and funds, Morgan James Publishing donates a percentage of all book sales for the life of each book to Habitat for Humanity Peninsula and Greater Williamsburg.

Get involved today, visit
www.MorganJamesBuilds.com

This book is dedicated to Xristos and Andrea.
You are forever in our hearts.

Also to all the mothers, mothers to be and to the women
who tried and never managed to become mothers.

Finally to the doctors and nurses who
perform miracles in their Neo Natal Units.

Table of Contents

Prologue

Throughout the ages, man was the dominant figure in the household. The woman would stay at home, clean, cook and bring up the children. The man would go out and hunt for food or as it is nowadays go to work and provide for his family.

A woman's role in comparison to before, is to go out to work, as well as do her daily jobs in the house. Her role as just the housewife has changed.

The only fundamental constant factor in all households, is the woman's gift and yearning of creating life. It is embedded in her genes. Being a mother is by definition, what makes a woman complete. It is the very essence of who she is.

~

"Not again! When is this nightmare going to end?" Tears stream down her cheeks and then the uncontrollable shuddering of crying ensues. Life just sucks! For years now, she followed every bit of advice she received. "Why does it not happen for me?"

Her husband comes over, with black clouds hovering over his head and a knot in his stomach. "Here we go again!" he thinks to himself. He cuddles her and tries to give her words of comfort.

Last time this happened he did not say anything and she lashed out at him, accusing him of not caring. "Don't cry baby, it will happen for us next month". He unintentionally lit a fuse.

"How can you say that? Have you got a crystal ball or something? Why are you still with me? I'm a freak. You should be with someone else who can give you what you want!" The stream of tears turns into a river. The husband feels like a punch-bag and is unsure of how to act or what to say. He does not talk and he is classed as uncaring. He talks and he is accused of talking rubbish. This scene is taking its toll on him. Here comes another month where he has to perform on command. Soon there will be the usual apologies and more tears. He wants his wife back. He does not recognize this woman. His wife is considerate, loving and witty. This woman is aggressive, unreasonable and she treats him like a human punch-bag. Is this desire of hers worth this hassle? Why does she not take a break and let her hair down? Have a few drinks and let him whisper sweet nothings in her ear, while he is leading her in the bedroom? Unbelievable! He still does not realize the depth of her desire to become a mother.

Do you recognize this scene? Are you one of those couples who are having trouble falling pregnant? Is it taking over your life? If you have never experienced the above, thank your lucky stars!

If you have, welcome to the club.

Every which way she tries, ends in failure. IVF is the only option left for her.

Injections, unreasonable arguments from the wife; hormones and mood swings all over the place. What keeps you going? Is it the hope that IVF will work for you and your wife will return to being her normal self again?

For your wife this is the last chance saloon. What she hopes is that with this extra help she will finally get to realize her dream and at long last become a mother. Your wife is willing to jump through any hoops and face any pain and danger in order to become a mom and create your family. Have you not yet understood how deep this desire runs?

A telephone call from the clinic, "None of the eggs fertilized". Tears of sadness and desperation engulf your wife. Welcome to the club of despair and misery. Even with IVF she cannot fall pregnant. Life sucks! Your wife needs your understanding and support more than ever before.

A telephone call from the clinic, "Sorry, you are not pregnant". Dear Lord, even with two fertilized eggs in her she failed at the last hurdle! It is a hard pill to swallow coming this far and failing. Be there for her. Be her husband and not just in words. This is a really very sad club to be in.

A telephone call from the clinic, "You are pregnant!" What joy and happiness! You have finally joined the ranks of pregnancy. Welcome to the club! Whether you reached this stage, falling pregnant the normal way or through IVF, congratulations! I hope yours is a normal, uneventful pregnancy and both your wife and baby come out of it healthy. Welcome to the club of euphoria and contentment. You deserve it. You have reached the beginning of the most noble of dreams; to create life—to become a family. Enjoy this feeling, for it can sometimes be taken away from you in the blink of an eye, through no fault of your own.

"We have to perform an emergency caesarean. Failure to do it now will put both your wife and baby at risk." The blood drains from his face. "No…" It is just too bloody soon. She is only just over five months pregnant. The odds are against them. He puts his faith in the doctors, for he believes in nothing else. The caesarean is performed and both his wife and baby are fighting for their lives. What started as a noble dream of creating life, turned into death, despair and misery! Do you recognize this scene? If not, thank your lucky stars. I never want to welcome anyone in this club. Whether you fall pregnant through IVF or the normal way, this is where hate, anger, misery and despair await you. This is where hope is lost.

~✧~

Since the beginning of time, women were blessed with the gift of creating life.

In the old days this great gift would put them in mortal danger, with many women dying whilst giving birth. Faced with this danger, did they stop? Like the true lionesses that they are they continued, helping the human race to continue to exist through the centuries.

With the advance of science, the risk of giving birth has decreased drastically. It can still be dangerous and fatal, but the death rate has decreased. However, their need to become mothers remains timeless, irrespective to the dangers to themselves.

Most women fall pregnant within a year of trying. Good luck to them. I hope they have an uneventful pregnancy and a healthy baby.

There is a sizable proportion of women, who suffer because they cannot make use of this great gift that they have. This soul sucking and gut retching desire consumes them to the core. They question their self-worth as it takes over their daily lives and stops them from enjoying life and those around them. Misery and sadness become their constant companion. It actually makes them question the reason for their existence. If they cannot become mothers, then what is the point of it all? The irony of this, is that this inability of theirs to fall pregnant raises its ugly head every single month without fail, taunting and tormenting them. Their desire and desperation are so great, that they are willing to try and believe anything. However stupid and far-fetched something is; if they think that there is even the slightest chance it might help them, you can bet your last dollar that they will do it. Their need is so great that it defies logic. Behind that determined and tough exterior, what exists is a fragile human being! They need our understanding, support and compassion, for their need is noble and divine.

Irrespective of how long they have been trying, how many ovulations charts they filled and how many recommendations from old wives' tales they followed, their ultimate goal still eludes them. Pregnancy taunts them and propels them to the realms of hopelessness. The one thing that defines them as a woman is the one thing that kills them a bit at a time. The one thing that can bring completeness in their lives is the one that is tearing their lives apart.

Men have to understand this and support their wives/partners who have trouble falling pregnant or are completely incapable of falling pregnant. This must be devastating for them. It is not enough to say, "Yes my love, I understand..." For these are just words. Men have to really get it. For a man to understand this, he has to assume that he is facing impotency or firing blanks. This is a killer for any man. If there is no cure, it can make any man suicidal. It is to the same extent that pregnancy and motherhood is precious to women.

The most recent medical advance in relation to this problem of theirs is In Vitro Fertilization (IVF). All sorts of chemicals are injected in them. Their hormones are all over the place and through this method a woman's menopause might come a lot earlier in her life. That's right, you guessed it! With all these negatives embedded in this method these lionesses are not only willing but thankful. Their desire is so great that their own safety comes a very distant second. These noble human beings put their own lives in danger every time they give birth. Yet, they are still there willing to do whatever in order to create life.

IVF has brought joy to a lot of families, which would have otherwise faced a childless future and a lot of tears. IVF has brought pain as well, for every method has its pros and cons. People who have had a successful result will sing the praises of IVF and people who have had bad results will of course condemn this method.

Before any of you embark on this journey, please, make sure, you read both sides regarding this method. Everyone who goes through IVF is hopeful that they will be successful. The reality is it can be a positive or negative scenario; with the odds for success tipping towards the negative. In general people have to undergo several attempts on IVF before they are successful. Sometimes though, however many times they try all they are left with are bank loans, an emotionally scarred and depressed wife and a husband who feels helpless in aiding his wife. Read about the negative views as well because it can happen to any one of us. I am not trying to scare you or put you off. What I am trying to do is to help you understand the whole picture. At least this way, if you fail your first IVF you have some idea about it and it is not totally demoralizing. It is not the end of your dream. You can try again providing your financial situation allows you to do so. You review your options and you soldier on. You do have options. You can still achieve your dream. It can be achieved after a lot of pain and suffering from your wife. Do not lose hope. The trick to this journey is compassion, support and understanding for each other.

The bottom line is, your wife is the one who has to go through having the injections, stopping her cycle and her hormones being all over the place. This very woman needs and deserves your unwavering and unquestioning support throughout this process. It is the least that she deserves for she is the lioness who is willing to jump through any hoops in order to create your family. Be there for her and put her on a pedestal. She deserves this and that's where she belongs.

The points that this book is trying to convey are these:

Celebrate women for they are the lionesses who create life irrespective of the dangers to themselves. The strong, unyielding desire of the majority of women to become mothers is timeless.

Those who fall pregnant, the normal way, good luck to you; for the unlucky ones who need help, the current method available at the moment is IVF.

Following the process of IVF; you have to understand that IVF does not give you any guarantees; couples have tried quite a few times before achieving their dream; others, even though they have tried countless times have not succeeded.

The emotional roller-coaster that women go through, as well as the men.

Whether a woman falls pregnant the normal way or through IVF, this book gives you a true-life scenario during pregnancy and after birth, full of despair, heartache and hope; it happened to us. I hope it does not happen to anyone else. The reality is it can happen to anyone.

Hi, my name is Steve and my wife's name is Vaso. We are your average couple, working and paying our bills. This is our story of wanting to have a baby. The procedures we went through and the disappointments. The successes we had and the pain and heartache. Our journey is one of pain, despair and hope. Through this journey you will get to read both of our accounts about this period in our life. Vas's version will be in italics.

The account we give here is our actual life story without glorification or exaggeration in order to make our journey more dramatic. It is all documented in the various hospitals that we had spent time in for one reason or another. We have really spent a lot of time in hospitals! Some dramatic facts were left out because they are private or we are too scarred to relive them. Baby steps! At least we are now able to talk about most of our experience.

Even if only one couple benefits from reading our journey we shall consider it a success.

This book is not focusing on just the IVF procedure. If you get lucky and you fall pregnant through IVF or the normal way, you are not out of the woods yet. You have to face the term of the pregnancy and giving birth. It might not be the smooth sailing we would all like it to be. Life has a way of knocking you down when you least expect it. We have been knocked down. Not once but lots of times. Throughout our ordeal, I felt we were a punch-bag taking blows constantly without any respite. Take courage and always try to get up and remain standing!

There are couples that do not want to have children. Good luck to them. It is their right and choice. We are all created different.

Life should not be, 'live and let live' it should be, 'live and help live'. It is more rewarding and fulfilling. If someone you know has problems conceiving, do not keep asking them, "Have you fallen pregnant yet?" You might be concerned but this is the wrong way to express it. Instead find out what the problem is, read about it and let them know you are always there for them, when they are ready to talk. If you are in a group and the topic of babies come up, do not shy away from the subject. There is nothing worse for that couple than to get pitying looks or conversation from their friends. Treat them the same as you would normally do. They already know they have a problem. Do not amplify it by tiptoeing around them.

Trying to fall pregnant, getting pregnant, and eventually giving birth, is part of our cycle of life on earth. What makes our story relevant to this scenario is that in all three of the above stages we faced difficulties and scares of immense proportions. By reading our story you get to see some of the things that can go wrong in all of the above stages; from just one family. Don't get me wrong. I am sure that other families have more harrowing experiences than us. It is just that we decided to tell our story and put it out there for people to read.

The idea for this book, started when I got home one night and saw my wife watching the news in tears. When I asked her what was wrong, she told me that she had just seen on the news a segment about a celebrity in England whom Vas likes. Her name is Amanda Holden and she is a TV presenter and a judge on Britain's Got Talent. She had severe problems with her pregnancy and had to be rushed to hospital. Vas was upset and said a prayer for her and her baby that night. A woman she did not personally know had made her cry and say a prayer for her. That's my Vas. Sensitive and loving to the core! I was touched by her reaction and also realized that shitty things do not only happen to people like us. They happen to everyone.

This is why we must share our stories, so that other people in similar circumstances can draw strength from them and think, "If they could overcome this then hopefully, so can we. We are not the only ones who have gone through such an ordeal." It might help them to avoid the mistakes we made and perhaps go through their tribulation with less pain than we did.

The main section of this book concentrates on a specific period of our life; one and a half year to be exact. That was the beginning of our dream, full of hope and promise, which turned into a nightmare of deaths and fighting for the survival of our very family. It was a period of anger, hate, helplessness and despair. It was a period that can test the mettle of any couple.

We have been tested severely.

Chapter 1
How We Got Together

The first time I met Vaso, was when I was on holiday in Cyprus, visiting my parents. I entered the dining room and I saw a group of people, I have never seen before. Introductions were made, which were irrelevant to me, as I usually made a quick exit. Their conversation was always about the good old days. After listening to a lot of them, I always tried to avoid them. However this time was different.

On the right hand side of the table, I saw a lusciously tanned black haired girl. My parents were surprised to see me hanging around and engaging in conversation. Their surprise turned to shock when they saw me actually take a seat around the table. Not just any seat. I squeezed myself, forcing everyone to move, so I could sit next to her. After chatting with the tanned girl, I found out her name was Vaso and she lived in

England, the same as me. She explained to me the link between her family and mine. Dad's brother was her parent's best man and godfather to her brother. I was mesmerized. I had no intention of leaving early. I found Vas (my affectionate name for her) quite captivating. She was so darned tanned from sunbathing. She was quiet, but she was also witty. I was interested and intrigued. She really made an impression on me. When I tried to talk to her, it was effortless. The banter between us was great. She worked as a bank clerk, while I was running a fish and chip shop (It is a hot food take away!). When the time came for them to leave, I actually felt quite sad. I wanted to get to know more of this sexy and witty girl.

It was not to be.

Due to just starting my own business, the loan payments, trying to attract more customers and fighting to stay afloat, kept me from pursuing her.

The following year, when they went to Cyprus for a holiday, they visited my parents again. This time, they asked if they could stay the night. They were taking liberties!

Later on, when I asked Vas, in which bed she slept in, I found out that she slept in my bed. I would like to think, that she wanted to leave her scent for me, for my next visit. I think she was besotted, but she did not know it just yet. I have that effect!

Steve is exaggerating here. I did not even know that that was his bed.

A couple of years went by and I received a call from my cousin informing me that she had just seen Vas and that she was interested in me. Well, I could not blame her, but the thing was…I was interested as well.

I was very close to Steve's cousins in England. We grew up together and the question came up about Steve. I smiled and his cousin took that as a green light for her to call Steve and sing my praises.

Our first date went like this; I met her for lunch on a work day. There we were, sitting at a table and giggling at silly things, like two naughty school kids. It was brilliant. When I joke I do not smile, which makes it difficult for people to get whether I am serious or not. Vas almost wet herself. I had found my audience. She was also funny and witty. I knew that very day that I wanted to spend the rest of my life with her. Obviously I did not tell her. I did not want her to get big headed. I walked her back to the bank and drove back home. I spent one hour with Vas and six hours driving; a small sacrifice to make when it gave me the chance to be around her.

Our second date was also memorable.

We went to see the film The 'Bodyguard' with Whitney Houston and Kevin Costner. We both drove there but I forgot to tell her that I did not know the area and that I would need directions when we left. After a few tears by Vas during the film, we kissed goodnight and we both set to get in our cars. She was parked 7 parking spots in front of me. My intention was to follow her until the main road. The night was rainy, windy and the visibility was atrocious, as the street lamps were few and far between.

I started to follow, whom I thought was Vas. To my horror she took off straight away without waiting for me to pull up behind her. She was also driving quite fast. There was nothing else to do, but follow her. She was turning left and right, going through a more populated area, which I did not recognize.

"Where is she going?" I thought to myself. Whatever speed she was doing and whatever turn she was taking I was right behind her. I could not afford to lose her, because I had absolutely no idea where I was.

Before you ask, there were no satellite navigation systems then nor lots of mobiles phones. It was the age when arrows were shot instead of bullets! We were not as advanced back then.

I was getting uneasy. I had a bad feeling about this. I decided to overtake her and ask her what was going on. As I pulled up next to her and raised my hand to signal her to pull over, what did I see? To my horror of horrors, that was not Vas. Instead, I saw a frightened girl, driving her car and was desperately trying to lose me. She probably thought that I was a stalker trying to do her harm. I looked away and pressed on my brakes, trying to take the first turning I found, praying that she did not remember my face, or got a glimpse of my number plates. Poor girl, at least, I put her out of her misery. I bet she spent the rest of her journey, checking her rear view mirror just in case I was still following her. I unintentionally scared the living daylights out of her. I just hoped there would not be a policeman waiting for me when I got home. Now I had problems of my own. The problem at hand was that I was utterly lost. I started taking random turns, hoping I would get lucky and find the main road. No such luck. Unknown to me I was driving further away. I should have reached home at 12:30 am. Instead I arrived about 3:00am in the early hours of the morning. The good thing was that at least there was no policeman waiting for me.

When I called Vas the next day, she could not stop laughing. She found it hilarious. I did not. She had and still has a quirky sense of humor. My life is richer with her in it.

I burst out laughing when he called me the next day to tell me what happened. I was chilling out at home with a cup of tea, while Steve was on a magical mystery tour! I really thought he knew where he was. I am sure he will not get lost around that area again.

I think one of the biggest gambles a man takes in his life, is the woman he marries. If you choose unwisely, you will either divorce or lead a life of misery and resentment. If you choose wisely, you lead a happy and content life and cannot wait to finish work so you can go home and be with your wife. I am in the second category, as every day I cannot wait to finish work so that I can go home and be with my Vas. I did not just get a wife but a best friend, a soul mate and an audience for my jokes!

This situation helps later on in life, when you are faced with adversities. Let us face it; at some point in our married life we shall face adverse conditions. If you are in the first category, you will throw in the towel and call it quits. If you are in the second, you face the adversities together as a unit and you soldier on. You are understanding, communicative and supportive. This is what I believe to be the most important ingredient in married life. I still cannot believe that I managed to get Vas to be my wife. People often wonder how we got together, as Vas is outgoing and I am quiet and moody! Well, Vas saw through the rough exterior.

Our courtship period was quite short. Nine months to be exact. We were married at a registry office on the 2nd October 1993. Vas moved up soon after.

I could not bear the miles Steve was driving every week. So I managed to get a transfer with the bank and we started our married life together as a couple.

Our church wedding was planned for the following year, on 26th June 1994.

The wedding was traditional. The sun was shining, people gathered from all over the country and Cyprus. Dad always wanted to walk his daughter to church, with the violins playing and him proudly holding his daughter's hand. There must have been at least a hundred people walking with us. The violinists at the front, followed by the priest, then Steve and his dad, then me and my dad, followed by everybody else. I was elated. It was really something amazing.

Unfortunately the photographer managed to upset Vas. He kept pronouncing her name wrong.

You would think he would manage to get something as the bride's name correct! All I could hear all night was him calling my name wrong. He really pissed me off. Apart from that though, I was on cloud nine.

The day flew by very quickly. We ate, drank and danced the night away with our loved ones. Everybody had a wonderful time.

We pretty much decided to start a family straight away. This was going to be great. Practicing was going to be fun. I was now married to the guy I loved.

It was sheer happiness and contentment for me. I knew I chose wisely. I could not believe how lucky I was. Life was just brilliant.

Chapter 2

Trying to Fall Pregnant

W e came back from our honeymoon full of dreams and determination. I just could not stop smiling, knowing that Vas was my wife. She wanted kids. It was okay with me. It was fun. There was an abundance of sex without any pressure. I was in heaven and quite earnest to oblige. Whenever we saw someone we knew their first question was, "Any babies on the horizon yet?" My answer was; that we were practicing and working on it!

I could not wait to have kids. I have always wanted three kids. Like most women, I pictured myself nurturing them, helping them grow up and guiding them through life. I wanted to be the mother hen. I wanted to give birth and hold my babies in my arms. Hear their first cry. Teach them how to walk, talk and cuddle them when they cried. Hear their laughter echoing around the house. Play with them. For me a scene like that was heaven. I just could not wait.

At the beginning I used to smile at their question, as I thought it was only a matter of time. At that time, it was not important to me whether we had a baby or not. My personal view was if Vas fell pregnant, "Great" but if she did not, I was okay with it too; it was not the end of the world.

However for women, it is different. I did not appreciate this at the time. It's their natural urge to become mothers. They feel a failure as a woman if they don't have a child. I just could not understand it. I kept telling Vas that it did not matter to me. She never believed me and insinuated that I should be with someone who would bear my children. How can you argue with that? You tell the truth about how you feel, but you are not believed. However, I was not concerned as we had only just started trying to get pregnant.

Who would have thought that having a baby was so difficult? I was so flippant about it. I even joked with my sister-in-law in Cyprus about it, "I'll race you" I said to her. The worst thing I ever did was telling the whole world that my husband and I were trying for a baby. Every month I felt like a failure. Family would ask me constantly, "Well, any news?" The answer was always the same, "No". My sister-in-law won the race…

Time does not sit still. Six months became a year. We were now officially classed as having problems with fertility (A woman under the age of thirty-five who has not conceived after twelve months of contraceptive-free intercourse). Needless to say, we did not know it at the time. A year became two years. We started married life full of dreams but this thing with Vas's fruitless efforts of trying to get pregnant sort of put a damper on things. I could see that it was weighing on her mind. It was devastating for Vas to see her irregular period month after month. Some months we were at it like rabbits. That did not help either. Too much sex, too little sex, it really did not make any difference. It was just not bloody happening. To be honest, it started to get me down.

You have to reach the end of your tether before you accept that you might need help. Well, we did and we decided to see our doctor. The way we were going we would be 70 years old, boxes full of Viagra and still trying!

When you are young, you plan in your head, a sequence of things that you want to happen in your life as you grow older. The things you plan from a young age, you expect them to happen as you had already seen them happen to your parents and friends. Get a job, a car, and a girlfriend. Get married, get a house and have kids. In your teenage years that sequence of events is expected to happen in a smooth and orderly fashion. For Vas and myself, this sequence got stuck at the very end and it showed no signs of resolving itself any time soon.

⌒◯

After trying for a long time, we decided to go to the doctor for help. It was not an easy decision to make; admitting that you need help, is a hard pill to swallow.

The dream was to surprise Steve with the news. To do a pregnancy test and see it positive. I wanted what I thought most people experience naturally.

I felt that I had failed Steve and that I was incomplete in some way.

I had to monitor charts, temperature plotting, drawing graphs and taking tablets (Clomid) with the hope that it would work.

It was like a science experiment. I followed everything that I was told to do, without any joy whatsoever.

It took over our lives, literally. Every thought, every day, from the moment you first open your eyes in the morning, to when they close last thing at night, was about that.

It controlled our lives. Nothing else seemed to exist or matter. We were in a bubble of, "Trying, trying, trying" and, "Nothing, nothing, nothing".

Performing on command, rather than when you are actually horny. There was no horny anymore. Sex (lovemaking) had lost its magic.

There was talk of ovulation and periods which I was not too keen to hear. A woman's body is a mystery to me and I don't mind if it stays a mystery until the day I die.

We went home and Vas was energized with a new resolve. She started making notes on a chart as to when she last saw her period, last time she ovulated etc. She would pinpoint as to when it was the best time to have sex which would increase our chances of falling pregnant. I was going to work while Vas was planning our optimal time for sex. Looking at those charts, it felt as if I was back at school and I was going to be marked for my performance. In this case, my penis (the general) as well as my sperm (swimmers). The general had to be ready to perform at a moment's notice, irrespective of whether I was tired or did not feel like it. My swimmers' success was to be measured by them managing to get my wife pregnant.

The first casualty of this new regime was for me to start wearing boxers. Apparently the other underwear I was wearing allowed no freedom and kept my balls squeezed and hot…which could result in low sperm count or tired swimmers. Go figure! At the time, I was not too happy about being told what underwear to put on. That day it was underwear, what would it be next?

I remember when I was younger, sex was the only thing that occupied the majority of my thoughts. When we first got married sex was the prevailing thing on my mind, too. I could not wait to go home and perform like a lion! Coming to this stage of trying to fall pregnant, with ovulation charts and commands of when I should perform, took the fun out of such a pleasurable activity.

What used to be exciting and spontaneous became quite regimental and mechanical. We had lists for this and lists for that. I exhausted my poor husband. He never said anything, but I could see it on his face sometimes that he was not very happy to perform on command. He would come home from work sometimes and I would be there waiting for him, telling him to come to the bedroom as I was at my optimal time of ovulation. I expected him to be ready at a moment's notice. At that time, I thought it was a small sacrifice to make on his part.

If you want to kill the desire for sex for a guy show him ovulation charts and tell him when he has to perform. Not the most romantic things to get you aroused either, I might add. The guy loses control. It's not when he wants to, but when he has to. It becomes so clinical.

Some days when I was really tired and driving home from work, I was under pressure because I did not know whether I had to be ready to perform as soon as I got home. So much pressure! You see, women just lie down, whereas the general has to rise on command, irrespective of whether I was tired or did not feel like it. Some days the general was tired as well and needed extra encouragement to rise to the occasion. It was just not fun. I felt like a puppet! Vas was relentless. That was when I first appreciated how important it was for her. Every time she would see her period a piece of her soul was destroyed. The vibrant, witty girl I knew was disappearing a little at a time.

⚬∕⚬

Every month…nothing; my damned period would rear its ugly head and torment me. "You are a failure. You cannot get pregnant. You are never going to be a mom".

Friends and family would keep asking every month, "Any news?"

Why, why couldn't I keep my mouth shut?

In the meantime, it felt like everyone around me was falling pregnant. Don't get me wrong. I was happy for them, but the pain I went through was excruciating. I would cry behind closed doors, but to the outside world, I joked and smiled.

It was killing me!

Priests were praying for us, in Cyprus, Greece and England. Ribbons, blessed by monks were worn around my waist for months. I would give anything a go. I prayed and prayed, "Please, please listen to my prayer. Just give me one chance. Just one chance to prove myself! All I want is to be a mom."

⚬∕⚬

Every damn month, was like being caught in a loop and we could not get out of it. It was disheartening and at the same time demoralizing.

We had tests and my swimmers seemed to be fine. That was a relief. I never expressed it and it might sound selfish but I was very proud that my swimmers were okay. I don't think I could have handled it if I knew that the reason we were not falling pregnant was because of me. I would have been forever thinking that other people would refer to me as the guy who could not get his wife pregnant. It's stupid, I know but that's how I felt. My manhood would come into question. We are quite sensitive as far as that is concerned. Men and their pride!

Vas had something with her ovaries which to this day I don't understand. We did not do human anatomy at school and about things I don't know, I really haven't got a clue.

⟋

After trying for so long to fall pregnant, I went to our doctor, who referred me to the hospital. After a detailed examination, they discovered that I had polycystic ovaries. That was the reason my cycles were longer than the usual twenty-eight day cycle. Mine varied from twenty-eight to sixty. They were quite irregular. Due to this condition my menstruation was irregular making it difficult to pinpoint as to when I was actually ovulating. Also, due to this, it was doubtful if I was even ovulating. Just my luck.

⟋

The thing is, when you have a specific problem it always appears in front of you, so that it never lets you forget. You watch television adverts and you are bound to see things about baby food or pregnant women. You watch a film and there is always a pregnant woman or a baby. You go to the mall and it's full of pregnant women and moms pushing their babies in their pushchairs. It's everywhere! Every time I saw them I would tense because I knew that Vas would be sad as to why it's not her being the mom. She was happy for them, but why would it not happen for her? She had so much love to give.

People we knew would call with their good news (that they were pregnant). She was excited for them but it was another stab in the heart.

We would go to a function and people we had not seen for a while would utter their first sentence, "Any kids on the horizon yet?" By then I wanted to punch the living daylights out of them. I knew that even though Vas would smile politely at their question, inside she would tense and the whole evening would be ruined for her. I am the type of person that unless I have something constructive to say, I keep quiet.

Shame they did not follow my philosophy. When you have nothing to say, don't say anything. Don't talk for the sake of talking.

When you are single every friend's and relative's question is, "When are you going to settle down and get married?" As if that is the ultimate ingredient in life. Obviously it's a personal choice.

Once you get married the exact same people will change their questions to, "When are you going to have a baby?" No thought as to whether you have problems conceiving or you just don't want to have kids. If you want to ask personal questions make bloody sure they are not hurtful and instead talk about football or the weather.

Once you have a baby their question will be, "When are you going to give a brother or a sister to the little one?"

All you want to say to them is, "Mind your own bloody business."

From my perspective, I think it's harder for the woman. Being a mom is part of the definition of being a woman. For most women not being able to be a mother is like a man not being able to get an erection or firing blanks. For that reason men should be more understanding! It is a sacred need and for that purpose, tread carefully and sensitively around the subject. Be supportive and cut her some slack…a hell of a lot of slack!

We went for years having sex according to the charts of ovulation. Trying to do it at the best time with Vas ending up having her head on the pillow and her legs up on the wall. She said it was to help my swimmers find her eggs without getting tired. Was that special or not? Even though my swimmers were okay, if they were anything like me, they would have agreed with her reasoning, in doing the job with as little effort as possible. It seemed that even with Vas's help, my swimmers needed a satellite navigation system to reach their destination.

⌒〜⌒

I was losing hope and it was hard to remain positive. I could not even fall pregnant under the doctor's supervision. Everybody around us seemed to be falling pregnant. We followed all of the doctor's recommendations but still nothing. I don't think Steve was impressed with the regimental sex, but bless him, he never complained. I could tell though that he was not happy. The thing is we had to follow through with the hope that it would work. Steve was like a sex machine (bless him) but there was nothing romantic about it. He just performed when necessary.

Imagine having to deal with the same disappointment month after month, year after year. The thing you want the most, is the one that kills you a bit at a time because every month the dreaded period would appear. It happens so often that you lose hope and you expect that it will never work for you. It happens for so long that negativity becomes part of your psyche.

A friend of Vas, from London, sent her a fertility doll. Apparently it is supposed to bring luck to the woman that has her and help her fall pregnant. Under normal circumstances I would have thrown it in the bin. I do not believe in that kind of rubbish superstition. However, we were in unknown territory now. However much we tried, pregnancy eluded us. We reached a point where we were willing to try and believe anything.

The doctors, friends and family would tell us to try not to think about it and it will happen. The woman's body will relax and she would fall pregnant easier.

What a lot of rubbish! How can you tell someone to stop thinking about the very thing that's eating them alive twenty-four hours a day? How do you expect them to stop thinking about the very thing that they want most in their life?

Easier said than done.

At the time I considered it a stupid advice...and still do. There is no point in telling a starving person to stop thinking about food. He is bloody hungry. Of course he will always be thinking about food. A better suggestion was to encourage us to immerse ourselves in a new hobby. This way, even for a tiny brief period, our minds might have been occupied with something new.

A couple we knew invited us to go out. A couple of days before we were to meet, the husband called me and while we were talking, he told me that they are trying for a baby again because his wife did not give him a son yet. What do you say to that? Here we were drowning in our own sorrows; he had a healthy baby daughter and he was upset that he did not have a son! Clearly not the best people to socialize with at that time. I never told Vas the real reason I cancelled the dinner. I told him that we could not go out as I was busy at the shop and from then on I tried to avoid being around them. He knew we were fruitlessly trying to fall pregnant. If he had an ounce of compassion or understanding he would never have mentioned that. I could handle it but I knew that Vas could not. The last thing you need around you when you are trying and failing miserably to fall pregnant, is people like him. I cut all ties with them.

We had to accept that we needed help. It was just not happening for us.

Now we reached the point where it was not the case anymore of how many kids we wanted. It was the case that we most likely would never become parents. The fear of Vas not being able to be a mom was weighing down on us and becoming part of our life. Seeing Vas sad made me sad.

The problem with her need to become a mother took over our lives. It actually stopped us from enjoying each other and the little things in life.

Before all of this, I was uncomfortable in listening or talking about periods. When a girl at the shop was not feeling well, she only had to start with the letter p…(Period!), and I would stop her from finishing the sentence and send her home.

Now I was a pro. I was immune to it. That was the one thing about women I hated. That was the thing that was destroying our life. Three years of feeling like a puppet! Three long years of seeing my wife sad.

My life revolved around my periods and ovulation.

Nothing else.

It takes over your whole life and it consumes you.

Instead of enjoying your marriage and your life, you get fixated on trying to fall pregnant and you think of nothing else. You want it so bad that you cry yourself to sleep every night.

It really is not a nice place to be in.

The transition from trying for a baby the normal way to IVF is not an easy one. When IVF was first suggested to us, Vas was not too happy about it. Women still feel inadequate that they can't conceive by themselves. They are such strange creatures! That's why I never managed to understand them. What difference would it make how she fell pregnant, as long as in the end she got to hold in her arms the thing she dreamt about her whole life? Surely the end result is what counts?

We continued trying with our negativity hovering above us.

The results were the same every miserable month.

Every month Vas would be late but still not pregnant.

Unfortunately it was a painful process that we had to go through for Vas to accept that we did not have the luxury of choosing how she was going to fall pregnant. It was not our call to make. These were the cards we were dealt with and we had to make the most of it.

The worst place to go to when you are failing miserably to fall pregnant is a Christening. Although you are happy for the parents and wish them well, deep inside you there is an angry volcano ready to erupt. Why does it not happen for you? Then there is always one idiot who will approach you and tell you that it is about time you had a baby as well. As if we were using contraception all that time in order not to ruin our social life! You go to such a happy event and you end up wanting to pick a fight with that idiot.

We had tried everything. Nothing worked. I felt a failure. I had to face reality. I was not one of those women who could just fall pregnant naturally. We really needed help. There was just no other way. It was difficult to accept it, but after so many disappointments, pride is knocked out of you. It was pride that prevented me from moving on. With pride gone and desperation taking over, I was ready to accept any new method.

I just wanted to have a baby!

Hitting the brick wall of desperation makes you accept that IVF is the only option. We hit that wall and we were finally mentally ready to accept that IVF was the way for us now. Well, the only way as we had tried everything else and failed miserably. It had been more than four years now of feeling like a puppet.

Here I would like to repeat the point I made earlier, about men understanding a woman's need to be a mom. Imagine you cannot get an erection. All you see around you is beautiful and sexy women. It makes no difference though. You might be the richest and most handsome guy in the world but you are still out of the contest. All the jokes we make in the locker rooms about the hot night we had the night before is like a stab in the heart for you. You can't have a relationship for the obvious reason. You feel you are not a real man. A woman can tell you that she loves you for your kind heart but you will push her away because the bottom line is, you can't give her what every other man can. You feel a failure and you live with the anguish every minute of the day. It applies to the same extent for a woman who longs for a baby and can't have one. We have to learn to understand that and be supportive.

I was supportive for the wrong reasons. I wanted Vas to fall pregnant because I was upset that she was upset. She is my wife. She is the beginning and the end! Alpha and Omega! Deep down it still did not matter to me whether I was a father or not. I was getting frustrated of seeing those damn charts and being ready to perform when I was told to and not when I wanted. Trying for such a long time was taking its toll. I just wanted it to be over with. I wanted my old life back. That was selfish of me, but that was how I felt. Fortunately I never told Vas how I felt. It would have made her feel worse about herself and put her under more unnecessary pressure.

I found out that my brother was going to be the godfather to the baby of a very close friend of mine from Cyprus, who never even told me that that they had a baby, never mind having him Christened. I called him later that day and he told me that he did not know how to tell me, as he was feeling guilty about telling me he had a baby, knowing that after trying for all those years we did not. I reassured him that it was okay and that I was happy for them. That was a compassionate and understanding friend, unlike the one who was upset that he did not have a son. The last thing I wanted was to make him uncomfortable or anyone else for that matter.

There are ways to talk about babies to a childless couple. The stupid way and the compassionate way. It takes all sorts of people to make the world go round. I just excluded from our lives people whom I thought were in the stupid category. By not having them in your life during your trying times in my opinion you reduce the level of unnecessary upsets during those times that you can do without.

I wanted to live in a loving and peaceful environment. I knew I was going to have that, when I married Vas. I did have it, after I married her. After our continued pathetic failures month after month, year after year, of trying to fall pregnant, a cloud of sadness sipped through our lives and we did not even realize it. We forgot how vibrant and happy we were at the beginning. This sadness became part of what we were. We were too stressed and consumed with the desire to fall pregnant that we did not realize the change in our bubble. When we met other people, they seemed to pick up on the change in us. We were not the bubbly couple they knew.

When I was at home though, we would talk constantly. When Vas called me at the shop, the average duration of a call would be about 30 minutes. This would be about twice a night. I think our closeness and feeling free to talk to each other about everything kept us strong. I would be on the phone to Vas and I would hear the bleep, letting me know that I had an incoming call. If it was a friend of mine, I would ignore it. Half an hour later I would call him back. The following day the same thing. My friends would complain that I ignored their calls and they were bewildered as to what I found to talk about with my wife, for so long. "We are trying to avoid talking to our wives and you prefer to talk to yours? You will be going home soon anyway. Can't she wait until you get home?" They thought I was weird because I was talking so much with Vas. I got married to hang around with my wife, not my friends. Our conversation was sometimes about serious things but most of the times silly and funny things. It did not really matter. My wife wanted to talk to me. I wanted to talk to my wife. That was enough. That was satisfying and rewarding. If I am classed as weird for wanting to do that, then I am proud to be weird.

Surely, this is the whole point of not being single and getting married? You want to spent time with your wife. I knew that we had our problems, with Vas not falling pregnant. I knew we were sad and it was taking its toll on us. But we were one and one way or the other we were going to persevere and carry on. If we were to get lucky and have a baby, then that was great. If we were unlucky and could not have a baby, then there were other avenues that we could explore, which we had already discussed between us (Adoption!). That was the whole point of us talking and communicating. It was an uphill struggle. It was tough going. I would like to think we were made of sterner stuff and we would bravely soldier on as a unit.

At the time I thought that was true. However sensitive Vas was; I was tough enough for the both of us. I was just naïve, as to the amount of scares and despairs life would throw at us. It was not a few but an unstoppable avalanche which came crushing on us. We did not stand a chance. I was not as tough and indestructible as I thought I was...No one is!

We were not greedy. We did not want fame and riches. We only wanted to have a baby and plod along life as best as we could. We were your average couple with our arguments like everyone else. We had our money worries. Normal everyday stuff.

Surely that was not too much to ask?

Apparently it was and if we were going to get anywhere close to our dream, there were penalties to pay. A hell of a lot.

The reality and despair of the situation, matures you beyond your years. It either splits you up or brings you closer than ever before. There are no half measures. At least in our situation, there were no half measures.

From this point on, our nightmares began. We thought that we had it tough so far. We thought that we suffered enough and that now maybe, we may get a lucky break and smile. We were actually hopeful whilst going forward to keep a date with terror. For it was utter terror. We began our journey full of dreams and hope while we were standing in quicksand.

The only positive thing that we had going for us was that we were close and loving to each other. When we got married and took our vows we both meant them. Good job, for terror was lurking round the corner and he meant business.

Our dream would have caused no harm to anyone, apart from bringing fulfillment and peace in our lives. We wanted to create life. So we came to the start of the next eighteen months of our lives, which brought with them anguish, death, despair and hope. That short period shook us to the core. It brought us on our knees. Where we thought we were strong, we were crushed. Where we were hopeful, we were terrified and despaired. Where we planned to create life, we encountered death and fight for the survival of our very family. Where we loved, I was consumed with hate and anger of immense proportions.

Life just sucked!

Chapter 3
First IVF Treatment

After a few years my doctor suggested going down the IVF road. I did not know anyone who had had IVF.

I had not ever contemplated such a thing. I felt that I failed my husband and that I was a freak. I hated myself. It took me a while to come to terms with the fact that this was a positive procedure. I read somewhere that IVF babies are special. They are more special because they are made with more love, pain and tears. They are <u>wanted</u> and loved before they are even <u>created</u>. They are planned and made with lots of love. Not as a result of a quick fumble in the dark. After reading this, I was convinced we were going to have IVF.

We were referred by our doctor to an IVF specialist at our local hospital. His name is Mr. Artley. As a first try his idea was to put my swimmers in a long syringe and inject them inside Vas and see what happened. Vas went over the twenty-eight days without seeing a period and we were cautiously optimistic. Then the hammer dropped. Vas saw her period.

The appointment was made to see the IVF consultant. They confirmed that I had polycystic ovaries and that my husband's sperm were okay. The consultant's assistant then told us in great detail the procedure that we were going to undergo and the necessary drugs that were going to be injected in me. It was a very detailed description of the process and quite daunting. We were told that if at any time we were not sure of something, to call them. However silly we thought it was, they explicitly told us to call them.

The first treatment was to take place, just after my 30th birthday. We had been trying for a baby now for more than four years.

We filled the relevant forms to actually undergo IVF. The cost of the IVF was funded by the National Health Service, as it was our first time.

When you read the literature about IVF you come to the point where it says that IVF babies are special. One thing they forgot to mention clearly is that the man is actually a spectator. Apart from ejaculating in a tube and having to put up with his wife's raging hormones, there is not a lot he can do.

The hard work is done by the woman.

Nonetheless, we would have still gone ahead anyway.

It is a marvelous advance in medicine that has brought happiness to lots of families who could not have children the normal way; we hoped it would do the same for us.

When you first talk with the consultant your spirits are lifted up. They tell you that the chances are not great as the process involves having to overcome various little challenges! There is a chance that your wife will not produce any eggs and the pain she went through was for nothing, which will also make her feel extremely bad as even with IVF she was incapable of producing eggs. If she produces eggs they then have to be harvested. They are graded as to their quality. That is the point where men do their one and only function. We ejaculate in a tube with the fear that when we are ready we don't miss and our swimmers don't end up on the floor. So much pressure!

They then pick the eggs of the highest quality. If you only produce one or two eggs of poor quality they will still be used as you have no other choice.

There then comes the nail biting waiting period. You have to wait to find out if the eggs have fertilized. If they have not fertilized then you deal with the heartbreaking disappointment; regroup and hopefully try again at a later date. If they have, they are then inserted into your wife and you are then faced with the final nail biting waiting period…to see if your wife has fallen pregnant. If she doesn't fall pregnant, she will need your support and understanding more than ever. It must be extremely devastating to have reached that far and fall on the last hurdle. If she falls pregnant; you are on cloud nine.

We were given syringes, needles and small capsules with white liquid in them. My first thought was; if we were stopped by the police, they would sure as Hell think we were drug dealers. Funny how the most stupid thoughts run through your mind at the most inappropriate moments!

The daunting part of this was that I was supposed to inject Vas with the needles, as we opted to do it ourselves instead of driving to the hospital every time an injection was needed. I am still not very clear of the purpose of each course of injections.

I was excited and scared at the same time. It was unknown territory for me. We opted to do the injections ourselves. My husband had the privilege of injecting the hormones.

Ouch!

Day three of my period I had a blood test to confirm that the required hormone levels were correct.

We started the treatment at day twenty one of my menstrual cycle.

I started my course with a nasal spray. Each day I would have to alternate nostrils.

The reason for the sniffing was to suppress my existing levels of hormones, for about two weeks. My body stopped producing hormones naturally. It is called the "menopause stage".

This meant hot flushes and mood swings.

What joy!

My mood swings were all over the place. It was not just that they were suppressing my hormones. The excitement of starting something positive. The fear that it might not work and having to face the daunting realization that I may be meant never to have children. I was a nervous wreck. I would lash out at Steve at any moment and for no reason. I could see the bewilderment on his face but I could not help it. He really got on my nerves. I found him quite suffocating at times. Later on, I would go to him with tears in my eyes, apologizing for being so terrible to him. The funny thing was he wasn't doing anything different to what he was doing before. Things that he was doing before and I found cute, were irritating the Hell out of me. Oh well, his life was not interrupted by the process, so a bit of grief was a small price to pay.

You actually lose control of your body.

The next stage was having the injections for ovarian stimulation. Steve was injecting hormones into alternating thighs daily. It is also called "super ovulation" which apparently may bring on early menopause

The reason for this is to grow several follicles. In a month you produce just one. This way it enables you to have lots of follicles.

Ovarian follicle

From Wikipedia, the free encyclopedia:

Ovarian follicles are the basic units of female reproductive biology, each of which is composed of roughly spherical aggregations of cells found in the ovary.

They contain a single oocyte (immature ovum or egg). These structures are periodically initiated to grow and develop, culminating in ovulation of usually a single competent oocyte in humans. These eggs/ova are developed only once every menstrual cycle (e.g. once a month in humans), a woman begins puberty with about 400,000 follicles.[1]

As a result I was hoping to have lots of eggs. The first injection he gave me felt as if he was cutting my skin. I was in agony. The tip of the injection was too thick. The following day we went to the clinic and they replaced them with smaller ones.

He was not doing it very well. The tops of my legs were a lovely shade of purple for a while.

Needless to say, there were lots of screams and shouts on my behalf and lots of panic and confusion on Steve's.

We finished the course of the injections and then Steve had to give me the final injection. It was to be given in my bottom. That was the worst. The needle was massive. The injection was given a few days before egg collection. The reason for this injection was to ensure that the eggs matured. Timing was of the essence. It had to be given at a specific time as stated by the doctors. No pressure then! I told him to be careful. It hurt like Hell. Some colorful words escaped from my mouth. I was not impressed.

Once that was done and dusted we had to go for the egg collection. I was very nervous as we were driving to Coventry.

There was a lot of traffic on the road and I was panicking, that we were going to be late. We arrived a little late but everybody there was lovely and calm.

We were taken to a ward where I changed clothes and details were taken.

I was put to sleep in theatre and for the first time everything was temporarily black.

As I woke, the lovely nurses were doing their observations on me and told me that they collected twenty-three eggs.

"What a result!" I thought.

Steve had to do his one and only contribution to this process. He said that he was under pressure not to miss. Dear God, give me strength. Are men stupid or what?

I had such a headache during that period. Vas would cry for no reason. She would blow up for no reason, or so I thought. My behavior was no different to before, so it could not have been me; I reasoned.

She craved dark chocolate.

I went out and got her ten bars.

That's all they had, for if they had more, I would have bought them all. When I got back, I got an earful because I got so many. She used to laugh at my jokes. Not only she wasn't laughing, but she actually asked me to stop telling her my jokes as they were getting on her nerves.

The injections were a bit painful. She was not impressed with my precision. It was a bit hard to inject smoothly as my hand was already shaking from the pressure and the probable screaming that I expected to follow.

Her hormones were all over the place. The only time I got a bit of peace and quiet was when I went to work. Whatever I did, I tried to think how Vas would react. Sometimes I chose to do nothing, as I thought that was the safest way. It wasn't. She would again complain that she had to keep telling me to do things. I just could not win; women and their bloody hormones. I never managed to make sense of them. They are different creatures to men.

You try to please them and they still moan!

That was not the sensitive, easy going Vas I married. That was a tough, irrational woman, whom I wanted to disappear so that the old Vas would come back. I keep saying about understanding and supporting your wife through this; however at the time, I was bewildered about the transformation and felt hard done by. Obviously I was not very supportive as in my own stupid way; I was trying to point out to her when in my view she was being irrational. It was as if I lit a fuse. She would then immediately lash out at me. It seemed to me that I was a punch-bag.

I had also my own insecurities to deal with.

That was not the way I thought I was going to create my family. I thought that when my wife fell pregnant it would be because I performed like a lion on one particular night and most probably kept going for two hours (Joke!). Here I was however, being asked to masturbate and place my swimmers in a tube. What a letdown. I also, always think of the worst. I was getting concerned that I would miss. Can you imagine Vas going through all that pain and the one and only job that was expected of me was ruined because I bloody missed? Knowing my luck, I wouldn't be surprised. So, there I was alone, trying to do the deed, with the niggling thought that I would miss. I was so proud when my part was successfully completed.

When I looked in the tube, I expected it to be at least half full as it had been a while. It hardly filled the bottom of the tube! When I told Vas later, she rolled her eyes. She was rolling her eyes a lot, during that period.

In a way, I began to understand her pain. When I had the 'flu, it was as if I was dying. I expected Vas to fuss over me. Man 'flu was the most unbearable illness or so I thought. I kept telling Vas jokingly, that only men caught that kind of 'flu, as women could not deal with it! She rolled her eyes at that as well. That was a very stressful period. I was walking on eggshells. Whatever I did or did not do, I got on her nerves. For me, it was a losing battle, for whatever I did it was wrong.

I could never make sense of women during those massive upheavals of hormones. I used to buy Vas flowers every week. One day, for an unknown reason, she was angry with me and she asked me to stop buying her flowers. So I did. The following week she was in tears. When I asked her what was wrong, she told me that I did not love her any more, as I stopped buying her flowers. I was gob smacked. When I pointed out to her that she told me to stop buying her flowers, she told me that she was testing me. Testing me for what? If she said she did not want them, then she did not want them. You cannot say something and mean something else.

This is why women drive men crazy, sometimes.

Just mean what you say and say what you mean. It is as simple as that. That is how men work. If you ask a man, "Do you want a cup of coffee?" and the answer is, "No" then it is a definite no and that is the end of it. If you ask the same question to a woman and she says no, that might not be the end of it. She might still end up drinking the coffee you made for yourself.

Vas would forever ask me what I was thinking. She credited me with a lot of thought. Most of the times my thoughts revolved around the next dreaded screaming volleys directed at me, food or simply nothing. I did not consider them as thoughts worth sharing, for I thought if I shared them, it would cause even more arguments.

I am generally a placid person and get on with everyone. I just did not know how to behave around Vas during that period: it was simply a nightmare for me.

I knew though, that once this was over, I would get the old Vas back; that gave me strength and kept me sane.

Later, we went home where I rested and waited patiently, for the phone call with our results. Two days later, we found out that out of the twenty-three eggs only one fertilized. Slightly disappointed, to say the least, but one egg is better than no egg.

Can you imagine that? Out of twenty-three eggs for only one to fertilize? This is the thing about IVF; there are a series of hurdles to overcome before you reach your dream. If you fall on any of them, you face the daunting task of starting all over again irrespective of how close you got to the goal the previous time. Well, one egg was better than none. I was devastated at the beginning, but truth be told, I got so far further with IVF, than I had the previous years. In trying to be positive and optimistic, I told myself that at least I knew for sure that I could definitely produce eggs and they themselves could get fertilized. Through IVF I knew for sure that I was not barren.

Two hurdles down…one to go.

Going in for the embryo transfer was not as daunting as I thought it would be. Obviously it was unknown territory for me, but I was forever praying, "Please God, let this work. Let me have my baby." My husband was awed by the way the cells multiplied. He is not very knowledgeable as to the workings of the woman's body or babies for that matter. Bless him.

The insemination was pain free and quick. You lose any form of dignity with your legs open and the doctor prodding through your privates. It is a small price to pay though.

Pessaries were given to me, to insert vaginally daily, to help maintain the "pregnancy state".

Then the all-important waiting game began.

The thing I remembered vividly was the last injection. It was massive. Vas's bum was sore. She screamed in pain…Oops!

Vas had her eggs collected. I did the one and only job that was required of me. I then embarrassingly, handed the tube with my swimmers to the nurse. I was so embarrassed! I knew that she knew what I had just done. I knew that she handled lots of tubes like that every day. Being a private person, the thought that someone knew for sure that I had just masturbated was very unsettling; I could not look her in the eye.

For the embryo transfer, we had to go to Coventry. As we had to drive through two motorways, we left quite early. It was stop and start. I don't know if it was panic that we were going to be late, but I had a bad feeling about staying on the motorway. So I decided to come off it and try to get to Coventry through the country roads. We had to be there at a specific time. That decision was correct, as there were long queues on the motorway because of a bad accident. We did manage to get there in time. I took that as a very good sign. Silly me!

What followed after that was the tense period. There was nothing we could but wait.

Nothing else occupied our minds.

We went through the motions of everyday life, pretending everything was normal, while inside, we were a volcano ready to erupt. We wished the days to roll forward, so we could find out whether it worked or not…

The waiting was the worst part of the treatment. The puncture wounds in my poor bruised legs were nothing compared to the waiting.

Two weeks after the insemination, I still had not seen my period. After calling the hospital and informing them, they gave us an appointment, where they took my blood to check whether I was pregnant or not.

I shall try and describe to you the mixed feelings that were going through my mind. Euphoria; that since I had not seen my period within those two weeks, there was a very good chance that I was pregnant. Fear; that given my history with long periods my body was going to give me the devastating blow, taunting me that I could never get pregnant. My mind was in such a mess. I did not want to be too positive, so as not to tempt fate.

On Monday the phone rang. I could not believe what I was hearing, "Pardon? I am pregnant? Oh my God…!"

Joy, tears, relief; we had done it! I felt so lucky.

First time.

Well done us.

As you know I have never been pregnant before. Whatever tests I did in the past they all turned out to be negative. After the confirmation that I was definitely pregnant, just for the sheer joy and to see how it looked on a stick, I took a pregnancy test. It was so satisfying to see. I had such a big grin on my face.

On Monday it was official. Vas was pregnant. I was ecstatic, for Vas was happy. At long last our ordeal was going to bear fruit. We were going to be parents. The world seemed to be a more loving place. My old Vas was back.

We were content and deliriously happy. All the stress and pressures of the previous years seemed to have just washed away. It was all a distant memory for me. Vas seemed to blossom. The laughter returned in our home. Looking at babies or pregnant women was a pleasure now. We were one of them. In roughly eight months, all being well, we were going to have our own baby.

Just like that, I got my old life back! Even though Vas was not feeling well, she was her old self again.

It's funny how unpredictable life is. One minute you are drowning in sadness and despair and the next you are on cloud nine. That goes to show you that we have to enjoy every scrap of happiness we get…for it can disappear very quickly, as it is so tenuous and fleeting.

I had very bad headaches and kept feeling rough. It was a small price to pay. I was on the way to motherhood! What joy! It was not until ten to twelve weeks into my pregnancy that the headaches seemed to subside and I started to enjoy my pregnancy more.

I bought maternity clothes.

I could not wait to wear them and show off my bump. I grabbed the experience by the gonads and ran with it. I bought baby clothes. It felt so surreal that there I was, buying baby clothes not as a present but for my own baby. I embraced pregnancy with excitement and passion.

We did not know the sex of the baby. We decided from the beginning if it was a boy to be called Xristos after Jesus Christ and if it was a girl to be named Maria after the Virgin Mary.

The first scan was supposed to pick up if there was anything wrong. They told us that everything was alright. I still could not fathom how they could tell the parts of babies in a scan. I tried to see but I couldn't. When the nurse tried to show me, I politely smiled indicating that I finally got it. I didn't. We went about the next few weeks with a big grin on our faces. We were going to have a baby. It was a pleasure to see Vas beaming with happiness. Even when she had headaches she was glowing. She did not think so, but to me she was. I have to admit that even though it was not important to me to have a baby, the euphoria of being around Vas during the early part of her pregnancy swept me away. I could not wait to be a father. I could not believe that I was actually instrumental for the creation of a life, even though my part in this was miniscule.

~~/~~

Regarding the name of the baby, tradition in Cyprus is for the first born, if it's a boy, to be named after the husband's father. In this case Petros, after my father.

I am not too traditional and as it made Vas happy, I was happy. He or she would be our miracle baby. Even I thought it was appropriate. I did not object. Just the relief to see her happy and not having to perform on command was enough for me.

The inevitable plans kicked in, as to how to decorate the baby's room. Vas's outbursts during the IVF procedure were a distant memory. I had in front of me the woman I loved in all her glory. She was her old self again and to top that I was going to be a father.

Life was great or so I thought.

~~/~~

I was approaching my seventeenth week of pregnancy. Presents were gifted and accepted. Everything seemed to be going well. I was going to my checkups, scans and blood tests; I took everything in my stride.

I remember the day clearly; the doorbell rang and I went to see who it was. It was my midwife. I did not think anything of her visit. I asked her in. We sat and I listened to what she had to say. She told me that there was a query with my bloods. "It could be something or it could be nothing, my dear. Try not to worry. I have made you an appointment for a scan tomorrow."

All the while she was there I was calm. I think I even managed a smile. Once she left I phoned my husband and I began to cry. Something was wrong with my baby. Oh my God, my baby!

The following day we had the scan. It was Friday 26ᵗʰ of June... Our wedding anniversary. We were then called in to see Mr. Artley the consultant.

"I am so sorry" he said, holding my hands "It is bad news..."

Everything from then on was a living nightmare. He told us that the baby had anencephaly. The baby's skull had not formed properly and that I had to terminate the pregnancy. I was given a tablet to kill my baby on my wedding anniversary. I was broken; destroyed. The world did not make sense to me.

There I was with my baby in my belly. There I was four and a half months before realizing my dream. I was in a small, windowless room, holding the pill in my hand that would terminate the pregnancy and my baby. The tears were uncontrollable. I did not want to take it. How could I be expected to do such a thing? My husband was with me, holding me tight. I thought I was losing my mind.

⟍⟋

We had the scan and then had a meeting with Mr. Artley to go over the results of the scan. We were told that our happiness was short lived. There was no chance for the baby to have lived, had Vas gone full term. The thing was, Vas was too far gone to abort. So, the only thing that they could do was to induce labor.

Can you imagine how devastating that was?

Here was Vas, coming close to achieving her dream of being a mother by falling pregnant against great odds. Now she had to go through labor and still end up without a baby! To actually feel the bump in her belly which she was caressing daily. To get through the first three months; to at last feel like a whole woman and for what?

It was as if someone was playing a cruel joke on us. I was numb. I remember there was a male nurse standing at the back during the meeting. I think Mr. Artley thought that I was going to run amok. He was wrong, for this is not who I am. I was more concerned with how devastated my wife was.

He was quite efficient and gentle in delivering the bad news to us. For that I am grateful. It must have been very difficult for him to have to give us those terrible words, "You must lose the baby..." He knew how desperate we were to have a baby. This longing and desperation can only be appreciated by couples who are, or have been unable to fall pregnant. Due to his profession, he saw that on a daily basis. For him to give us the good news that Vas was pregnant and then having to give us this deadly blow must have been difficult.

There in the room, Vas turned to me with tears in her eyes, telling me that we were destined to be just the two of us. To hear and see my wife in such a state was horrible. I hugged her and told her that we would get through that. They were empty words for I did not know what else to say.

Mr. Artley gave us a tablet for Vas to take which would induce labor. It generally took twenty-four hours to work. The two of us went in an empty room for Vas to take that tablet. She did not want to take it. She was crying. How could they expect her to do such a thing? I have never seen another person in such anguish and despair. Here she was, so close in realizing her dream of being a mother and now she was expected to swallow a bloody tablet which would kill our baby and our dream. There was nothing else I could do or say. It was out of our hands.

Misery and despair had engulfed both of us. I was full of hate and anger: the injustice of it all; the cruel twist in our fortunes; seeing my lioness crashing down and devastated.

Knowing that the brief laughter and happiness we had experienced, since we found out she was pregnant would vanish and be replaced by depression. You feel broken and defeated and that is what we were. I wanted to let out an almighty scream of anger at the cruel joke that had been played on us. I knew that Vas's spirit would be broken after this. Who wouldn't?

After a lot more tears and soul-searching, Vas tried to take the tablet. She would bring it near her mouth but she just could not put it in, as if there was some invisible barrier preventing her from doing so. She was bawling her eyes out. She would again bring the tablet near her mouth and stop. This went on for a while. I did nothing. It had to be her decision. I knew she had to take it but she had to do it for herself. Whatever action she took, I would have been there for her come what may. I was all cold inside. You have to walk in our shoes to begin to understand the level of sadness and desperation we went through; the cruelty of it all. That moment in time was soulless, cold and life had no meaning; our life just dissipated into a series of endless nothings. The day before we were flying high and that day we came crushing down. All this in twenty-four hours! How the Hell do you cope with such a drastic change in fortunes? How do you keep motivated to keep carrying on?

There we were in a windowless room. How appropriate. I was scared and life did not make sense to me anymore. It was a tiny vacuum, a void. The only way I can explain it, is the donkey and the carrot scenario. The carrot is dangled in front of the donkey teasing him and taunting him. He tries to bite it as it looks so near but however much he tries, he is unable to take that bite. It is so near, yet so far away. When he is about to get it, it is taken away. That was me. With shaking hands I finally took the tablet.

We went home and called my in-laws. Bless them, they left straight away and were with us within four hours.

When I decided to get married, the in laws never came in the equation as my view was, if I did not get on with them I would simply try and avoid them. I married wisely and the icing on the cake was that my in laws were great. You never get to appreciate them until you really need them. When I called my father-in-law, his first response was, "We are setting off right away…" No second thought about his business or anything else.

It was <u>Saturday afternoon</u> and Vas did not want to stay home and wait for the dreaded labor. Vas and her mom went to the hospital and asked if she could check in. Her room was ready. When I finished work I went to her. A lot more tears followed, for we knew what was coming and it was not good.

I was in hospital having contractions. I was about to give birth and I was bawling my eyes out. When a friend or family goes to the hospital to give birth, you wish them good luck with the pregnancy. There were no such wishes for me. I was given an epidural, gas and air. The pains started. There was no excitement for the birth. Just tears, pain, misery and a rising depression.

All day Sunday I was in labor. It happened at two minutes past twelve <u>Monday morning</u>. I could not have anticipated, even in my wildest nightmares that this scenario would happen. From starting the IVF to falling pregnant and burying my baby in such a short time.

Part of me died that day, as well. When the baby came out they told us he was a boy. He was dead. His name is Xristos and I would like to think, he is up there with the angels. He is my angel.

I had to watch Vas go through the tormenting pain of labor, with both of us knowing that we would not be taking our baby home. Instead our baby would be born dead. I had to see my wife go through the heartbreaking pain of giving birth. You see in documentaries and films, the husband standing by his wife offering her support, asking her to give one more push or how great she is doing and that he can see the head of the baby and so on…They both know that after the ordeal, they would get to hold their baby, hug each other and kiss with tears of joy in their eyes. Why the Hell, could we not be like them?

What I knew was coming was my dead baby and a devastated wife who would carry the scars of this ordeal for the rest of her life. Before we had the pain of trying to fall pregnant; now it was also the devastation of going through this process as well. That was not fair or just. I was never religious and never really thought about it. That day solidified my belief that there was no God; I became an affirmed atheist, for no just and benevolent God would play a cruel joke like this on us. Vas still held on to her faith.

There we were in the delivery room, Vas pushing and in agony. The tears that were streaming down her cheeks were not from the pain, but for what she knew was coming.

Our dead baby.

Our angel.

There I was standing by her side not knowing what to say or do. I was there in body; but in spirit I was in a dark place all by myself. I guess Vas was in her dark place as well. Our dead angel finally arrived in this world. DEAD. Our Xristos came without a cry and without a life. I held my wife tight. She was sobbing her heart out. Instead of being all smiles and happy, we were witnessing the death of our flesh and blood.

Where do you go from there?

There was only one place for us to go.

A few days later we were standing in the cemetery burying our dead baby Xristos. We brought our priest who performed the burial ceremony.

Vas was inconsolable.

We interred our flesh and blood without getting to know him; without hearing him laugh, cry or talk. Instead of taking him home and help him grow up, we were putting him in a box and burying him. The world was a dark place for us.

Just like that, our life changed.

We were devastated.

Wanting something so bad and getting so close to getting it, it's the hardest pill to swallow when it is suddenly taken away from you.

I know I am a flawed human being and most probably deserve to suffer. I get that and accept it. Vas however, is the kindest person I know. She is giving and sees the best in people. She is religious. What had she done to deserve this devastation?

The laughter that briefly existed in our home disappeared.

Of course now we had to deal with the sympathy calls.

Looking back, I get that everyone was trying to show their support. Back then I was not so understanding. Remember, I am flawed. I just wanted us to be left alone, as every call would take Vas back to the moment where she gave birth and start crying again. They would say, "Don't worry. It will work next time. I know it will." How the Hell, did they know that? Did they have a crystal ball or something?

The thing was, after they finished their call and got on with the rest of their day, my wife was still crying for hours. Even though they meant well and they wanted to express their sympathy and support, they were actually causing us more grief.

Life after losing Xristos was very dark. I was extremely angry and lost all faith and hope in the world. My life felt pointless. If I couldn't be a mother, then what was the point of carrying on? Literally.

I would go down to the cemetery and cry and cry.

I would hold my tummy and mourn my loss.

I hated not being pregnant.

To bury your baby, who you craved for, yearned and loved so much; it is truly the worst thing imaginable.

This wasn't part of life's plan. I didn't know anybody else who suffered a loss like this.

One moment I was on one of life's highs and then was smacked back down. I was an emotional wreck.

The thing I also found hard after giving birth to Xristos was the telephone calls from friends and family. Every time someone called, it took me back. I would try and hold it together while the conversation was going; but as soon as I put the phone down, I would cry for hours. It got so bad, that when Steve was at home and someone called, he would immediately tell them that I was not in. He would then end the conversation quite quickly. Sometimes he would not even bother to tell me, that so and so called. From his perspective, he was trying to protect me.

Well, I took my anger out on the wallpaper and basically stripped the house bare. It was a big task and it kept me occupied. It was actually quite therapeutic. I started the job like a woman possessed. At least it kept my mind occupied and even for short periods, it stopped me from remembering. As Steve always says, "Baby steps". Steve did not look to be greatly affected by the outcome. He does not easily show his emotions. I knew though, that he was hurting.

I am his wife after all.

This ordeal had actually shaken my whole being to the core. I was quite a vibrant, chatty and happy person. I turned into a recluse. My confidence had disappeared. To put it simply, I was a wreck. I felt I was a failure to my husband and the son I did not deliver alive in to this world.

We had a few days away in Jersey, which was lovely, but, my heart wasn't in it. Going over to Jersey was a different story. We got caught in the tail end of a hurricane, which was horrible. Everyone on the boat was very sick and the journey, which should have taken an hour and a half, took six hours.

That was a great year, I thought to myself.

When we got back from our little adventure, Steve thought about trying IVF again. I was still mourning the loss of Xristos and to be honest, I wasn't really bothered about going for it again. Not so soon anyway. I wasn't ready, physically or mentally.

How do you pick up the pieces and get on with the rest of your life? How can you smile when your wife is crying at home?

In all the literature we read, we had never read about a scenario like this. Don't get me wrong. That had nothing to do with IVF. We were grateful to have fallen pregnant through IVF. We were lucky to have a caring doctor like Mr. Artley as our consultant. We were just unlucky. In addition we were going to be first time parents, lacking a lot of experience in dealing with a grief like this. We are different in this respect. Vas is extremely sensitive whereas I am hard as nails. I have mellowed a lot since I met Vas. She brought a bit of my sensitive side within reach. Baby steps!

I am quite practical. I don't dwell too much on the past. I go over the mistakes I made, I make sure not to repeat them again and go on. That is who I am.

The problem at hand was that Vas was devastated. There were not a lot of things I could do for her, to ease her pain. Kind words and being there for her were all well and good. I felt that it was not enough. I just could not stand by seeing my wife in such a state. She was a shadow of her former self and it was breaking my heart to see her like that. I just had to do something! Anything!

It may sound selfish, but I wanted my wife back. I wanted to see her laugh and be witty. I wanted to see her happy. By wallowing in our own misery we were not taking a step forward. I was going to work while Vas was at home by herself crying. I had to do something. Well, I did!

Right or wrong, I had taken the decision. No one was going to change my mind. I thought I was clear-headed and practical and that was the only viable option for us. My wife was in pain and I was damned if I was going to stand around doing nothing.

They say the road to Hell is paved with good intentions. Well, my intentions were good. They were very good and pure.

The fact that I was naïve and stupid is beside the point. I thought that by making the decision, I was taking charge of my own destiny. I was stupid and as a result my wife paid for my mistakes, however honorable and well intentioned they were. Should I later find out that she suffered in the long term because of me the guilt will eat at me for the rest of my life!

How I wished I did not come off the motorway that day and we were late for the embryo insemination! At least that way Vas would have only been upset that she did not get the chance to fall pregnant instead of having to deal with what actually happened.

For every decision we make in our lives, there are consequences.

I was about to face mine.

Chapter 4

Note to Husbands/Partners

T he IVF road is a long, flat motorway-like roller-coaster, lots of
lows and very few ups but plenty of cork-screws in the belly.
You have to be prepared for it, accept it and deal with it; for
your wife's sake as well as yours. Your wife will be acting irrationally...
according to you. You don't charge like a bull in a china shop. Take a
deep breath. Then take another. Keep taking deep breaths until you
start smiling. Believe me, this is the most sensible thing to do. Her
body is pumped with all sorts of chemicals and her hormones are doing
somersaults. Most of the times she can't help the way she reacts; things
that you used to do and she found cute, may be irritating the Hell out
of her now. She will cry for no reason and lash out for any reason. This
is not a boxing match.

All you have to do is ejaculate in private in a tube.

That is your one and only contribution. She has to do everything else. Receiving a bit of unwarranted grief [A LOT] is a small price to pay. Do not continue the argument. Give her a cuddle or walk away. In ten minutes she will come to you in tears, apologizing for the way she acted anyway. You will hear lots of apologies throughout the whole process, for there will be a lot of unreasonable arguments. Accept it and deal with it, for if you are lucky and she falls pregnant, in nine months you will be holding your baby in your arms. This is the whole reason you embarked on this journey in the first place; to produce your own miracle.

Don't get me wrong. The advice I give here comes from the mistakes I made in dealing with Vas's mood swings. I am telling you this with the benefit of hindsight. We had our arguments, when I thought she was unreasonable. I did not back down or walk away. After quite a few of those, I came to realize that she could not help it sometimes, acting irrational. It was out of her control. I then came to the inevitable conclusion that the arguments continued because of me. I was not backing down. I failed to realize, that Vas was going through this motorway-rollercoaster and having to deal with her own private Hell. I considered life to continue as normal. You see, for me nothing changed. It sure as Hell changed for Vas. The mere fact that she did not go on about it, gave me the impression that that the status-quo was the same. I was wrong. When men are ill, we make sure our wives know full well about it. Women deal with it better with not as much moaning as men do.

I know our contribution to this process is miniscule. Before or after the IVF you can discuss your point of view. During IVF you do not bring this up. She has enough to cope with, without having to deal with your emotional baggage. Do not forget the hormones and chemicals that go in her body. We still don't know the long-term effects those will have on her. But she is still there and willing to take them, irrespective of the potential dangers. Understanding and support is the least she deserves.

Women are our lioness and the creators of miracles.

If there is something wrong with her and that is why she can't conceive; then this is why you chose the IVF route. When she is feeling down or her hormones are all over the place because of the injections and you feel frustrated and unjustly suffering, you should NEVER throw it in her face. She is probably already tormenting herself about it and the last thing she needs is for you to voice what she is already feeling. It is no longer that she has a problem or you have a problem. You are one now. You are a unit and you are trying to create a life. Act like one and your life will be richer for it.

Chapter 5

Note to Wives/Partners

Y ou are blessed with the gift of creating life. If you conceive through having sex we would like to think it was a night of passion unlike any other. We would like to think that it lasted at least two hours! We would also like to think that we performed like lions and the angels wept by our performance.

However going through the IVF route all that is expected of us is to ejaculate into a tube and hand it to a nurse. She knows what we have just done and with great embarrassment we hand her the tube. That is our one and only contribution in helping to create our family. We might not say anything but having to do only this, emasculates us. Thinking that other men might think, you cannot get pregnant because something is wrong with us, is terrifying. It is not a one sided sacrifice. Women have to realize what men go through. The worry and pressure, not to miss and get our swimmers in the tube is immense!

Throughout the IVF process you will be close to being unbearable. Your mood swings and lashing out for no reason will be numerous. We shall try to be understanding and supportive, even though we might believe you are acting crazy. Repay us with the same understanding and support. We don't understand hormones, as they are alien to us, but there will still be understanding...

Men come across as tough. Any negative mention regarding our manhood will result in World War III. We are extremely sensitive about it. There are two possible scenarios:

Our swimmers are not up to scratch; this will be devastating for us and you should never throw it back in our face at a time when you feel low or frustrated. This is a 'no go' area. We will feel inadequate, as you cannot fall pregnant, solely because we cannot impregnate you. The last thing we want to hear is you, voicing our shortcomings. You are criticizing who we are. The same way you expect your other half to be understanding and supportive, you should be the same. We shall forever think that people are talking about us, as the one who can't get his wife pregnant.

The other scenario is when our sperm are fine. Do not forget that, that is our one and only contribution. This pales into insignificance to what you have to go through. This is a bit emasculating for us as well. You might think it is silly; Men and women think differently.

Imagine when your boy or girl is born. When he/she asks you how he/she was conceived, you will tell him/her of your ordeal through IVF. When we are asked all we can say was that we had to masturbate. Not a glowing contribution to the process, is it? For us, it is not very manly. Accept us for the simple creatures we are. The same way you want men to be understanding, you should try to do the same. Be a unit. Become one.

Chapter 6

General Points

I VF is a road taken by many now. Whether you are rich or poor, it is a hard road to be on. Problems with fertility do not distinguish between race and color. It's a road taken by couples who have hit the brick wall of normal pregnancy to only be bounced back and smashed.

Unless you are both totally committed to it, think long and hard before you embark on this journey. Don't be one of those people who think that it will be a walk in the park. It will not. If everything goes okay, the only hard part is the beginning with the injections and the woman's mood swings. Once she falls pregnant it should be like any pregnancy. Here is the tricky part. Your first try might not work. Be strong and talk to your other half and jointly decide when you should start the second IVF. Listen to each other and don't try to force your idea as to when to start. You will understand what I mean by this later on.

In some exceptional circumstances you will have complications that you could not have envisioned in your worst nightmare scenarios. This is where you should be one and be there for each other no matter what. Be strong, supportive and understanding of each other. These are the qualities that will see you through and bring you closer together. You will see what I mean by this later on, as well.

Whether you fall pregnant the normal way or IVF, the scary times we have been through, can happen to anyone.

Chapter 7
Second IVF Treatment

A few weeks went by and I made up my mind that we should get on with the second IVF. At least this way if Vas fell pregnant again, it would lessen the pain of losing Xristos, as she was going to be focused on her new pregnancy. Well, that should have worked in an ideal world. (In fantasy land!) Here I made a big mistake…I should not have rushed us to have the second IVF so soon after Vas's ordeal. Here is where men and women think differently…

For me, even though it was devastating, the practical thing was to go ahead immediately. There was no point in dwelling on what had happened. What happened has happened and there was nothing I could do about it. I failed to take into account Vas's emotions. Mentally, she was just not ready. She was still grieving our lost baby. She was and still is an extremely sensitive person. She just was not ready and I railroaded her into having the second IVF too soon. I would not accept 'NO' for an answer. She did not have the strength or confidence to stand up to me. I was taking charge of our destiny or so I miserably thought. For the first time in our married life, I was ready to overrule her if she decided against it. I thought I knew best. There I failed miserably and let her down.

Steve was quite adamant that we should go through the second IVF soon after. My heart was not in it. I was not in the right frame of mind. I was still grieving. I was still healing. I was just not ready. I am not like Steve. He is tough. I am not.

There are no quick fixes when you go through an ordeal like this. This is why Women are from Venus and Men are from Mars. It was okay for Steve to say that we should go ahead. He went to work and came home in the evening. His only contribution to this process was to masturbate. It was me who had to go through the injections, sniffing, pessaries, etc. It was me who had her hormones off balance. It was me who was still grieving. It was me who was not ready. I was not strong enough to voice all this. That was around the time when Xristos was supposed to be born. Instead, I was starting my second time of IVF.

With the first IVF I was positive, but with the second I was not. I went through the treatment, but my heart and soul was still grieving.

I was spending a lot of time at the cemetery, with Xristos, talking to him, crying and complaining. I felt that the whole world was against me and I just needed to escape. I felt at peace with Xristos and I needed to be there with him.

On one particular day, during the sniffing days of the IVF, I had one almighty hissy fit and ended up at the cemetery, complaining to Xristos about his annoying father. Steve had gone to the pub, to negotiate about selling one *of our fish and chip shops. All I could see in my head was him having a jolly good time, while I was at home by myself suffering. I saw his newspaper, the weekend Financial Times, on the table beckoning me to come and play. Steve has this annoying habit with his newspapers. He leaves sections of it all over the house making it look untidy. He even keeps a section in the toilet! I cannot remember the times I told him to keep them tidy in one place. Normally, I would roll my eyes and tidy them myself. So seeing the paper's sections scattered all over the house, I snapped.*

I gathered them all and I took each leaf of paper and I shredded them; every single page, including a couple of magazines. It took me a while and I made a lovely pyramid in the middle of the living room.

Once that task was completed, I walked to the cemetery and sat with my baby and moaned about his father. The light began to fade a little bit and I decided to walk back home.

Steve had come home in the meantime. All he found was an empty house and the pyramid in the living room. He immediately got in his car and started to look for me. He was worried, bless him!

I sensed that I was going to run into him, on my way back and I did. I totally blanked him. It took him ages to convince me to get in the car. I continued walking in the meantime, while he was driving slowly, next to me asking me to get in the car. If there was a policeman around, he would have been arrested for curb crawling!

Needless to say, the next day I was extremely apologetic, but on the Sunday, the menopause monster was truly reeling its ugly head.

∽∕∾

We had our second IVF which was in Aldridge in West Midlands. It was more or less the same procedure; needles, syringes, etc.

It was November the 2nd. It was roughly around the time Xristos would have been born, had Vas gone full term. Instead of giving birth to our baby, she was putting flowers at his grave. I should have talked to her about it. I should have been a more attentive husband. I should have been listening to the words she was not voicing. I should have…

I was selling one of our fish and chip shops at the time. I arranged to meet the buyer at our local pub on a Sunday afternoon. Vas knew all about it. I had the meeting and after agreeing the price and a couple of pints of beer I went home. To my horror, there in the living room, one of my Sunday newspapers was torn to pieces and put in a pile. When I questioned Vas why she did it, her response was that she felt deserted by me as I was out having fun. I was gob smacked.

The next day, Vas apologized to me. There was no need; all I ever wanted was for her to be happy. She is my wife!

At the end of it, Vas's eggs did not fertilize. It was a devastating blow. Perhaps we were not meant to have kids. I started to believe that we were one of those couples that would be great aunts and uncles but unable to be moms and dads.

Our life was doom and gloom.

The bottom line is I should not have rushed Vas into it so fast. We should have communicated better. I should have been on the ball, as I was more clear-headed. I failed her as I railroaded her into it. I do hope the injections she had through this second IVF do not have any lasting long term effects.

—⁄—

Steve only remembers the incident with the newspaper. There were other things that he did which got on my nerves. For him it was life as usual. He tried to cheer me up with jokes that I used to laugh at before. God, they were getting on my nerves.

Even though none of my eggs fertilized, I was not that upset. First of all, I was not mentally or emotionally ready for the second try at IVF. It was just too soon. Secondly, I managed to fall pregnant once with IVF. So falling pregnant again was not impossible. If it happened once, it could happen again. I think Steve was more upset than me. Sure, my hormones were all over the place and my legs were bruised from the needles. Inside me though, I was confident that with God's help, I would fall pregnant again.

Christmas was around the corner and I told my family that I wanted to be left alone with Steve. I did not want any visitors, presents or decorations. I just wanted to be cocooned in my house with my husband.

Just before Christmas, the phone rang in the early hours of the morning. It was the police. Our shop had been broken into. It was a mess. Everything was smashed up, but Steve, bless him, was more concerned about how I would take it.

I realized a very important thing that morning. As long I had Steve in my life, we could get through absolutely anything. When he asked me if I was okay, I just looked around the shop and told him that it was not as bad as it looked. It was mainly superficial. With a lot of hard work and dedication, we managed to open the shop for business in the afternoon of that same day. We make a pretty awesome team.

⌒⌒

In a way this lesson had taught us to be more communicative. Especially me. We talk about everything now and any decisions taken are joint, without pressuring each other. However, Vas was the strongest here. She felt that since she fell pregnant with Xristos the first time, it could happen again. She felt it was a matter of time. She fell pregnant once and she was confident that it could happen again.

If any of you have the bad luck of the IVF not working the first time, I urge you to talk with your wife. There are no quick fixes. Give her time to deal with the disappointment and be there for her. When she is ready physically and mentally, she will let you know. After all, it's her who has to go through the process; you are physically just a spectator besides helping with the injections and creating the sperm in a tube.

Do not make the mistakes I made. Boy, I made quite a few of them. Hopefully by avoiding the mistakes I made, your journey will be easier. My heart was in the right place, but my reasoning was flawed. I recognized my big mistake and the unnecessary torment I put her through. I was never going to repeat it.

I am not talking about the financial cost. Vas had an unnecessary course of IVF chemicals injected in her through my stupidity. What long term effects that will have on her, time will tell. I shall have to live with the guilt that I harmed the person I love, by forcing her to do what she was not ready to undertake. Our position was that we would continue on the IVF roller-coaster, until we could take it no more. There was therefore a third try on the cards; the second try was a waste of time and it was entirely my fault.

By just admitting that it was my fault, does not mean anything. It's just words. I am sorry about it. I am extremely sorry. However, it had no effect on me, physically. Vas was the one who bore the consequences of my wrong decision. Through my arrogance, instead of helping her, I hurt the person I love the most in this world. These are not just words. It is a sincere apology. I know that Vas feels that there is no need. She is that kind of person. I feel that as we embarked on this journey to tell our story, I should admit my mistakes and make my apologies as well. There were a lot, but you will get to read only a few. I shall only deal with the big ones.

We were due for a lucky break or so I thought. We have been chasing this dream for almost six years now. Surely, we have paid our dues and we might get lucky!

When I got married, I was cocky. I had Vas by my side as my wife and I thought I would sail through life nice and easy. I think my cockiness was hiding my stupidity and naivety regarding joining the ranks of married couples and the tribulations that come with it.

That cockiness disappeared. I emerged as a conservative husband trying to remain afloat and taking care of his family. The reason I said afloat, is because there was a tsunami coming our way and I was completely unprepared for it. I was full of hate and anger. Why could it not work for us?

WHY?

Chapter 8

Third IVF Treatment

With a stiff upper lip and all that, we made arrangements to have the third IVF treatment at the Queens Hospital in Burton-upon-Trent. This time we talked about it and we were both in agreement. As usual Mr. Artley was there. He is a Middlesborough FC supporter but I do not hold it against him.

Same procedure as before; I will not bore you with the details as I am still not sure on the sequence. Even on our third attempt Vas had to explain the details again and tell me what to do.

This time eight eggs were harvested.

I did my only contribution to this process and again embarrassingly handed the tube with my swimmers to the nurse. I could never get used to that, as I knew the nurse knew what I had just done. Vas was going through all those invasive procedures, where one's dignity goes out of the window and I was uncomfortable about a nurse I have never seen before and most likely never will see again, knowing that I have just masturbated. Go figure!

Having IVF is no guarantee you will fall pregnant.

That's why they put two or three eggs in a woman, to increase the odds. We had two eggs inserted. We were cautiously optimistic. Knowing our track record we did not hold much hope.

I felt the universe was against us.

Vas was the optimistic one.

My poor mother, who lives in Cyprus, was lighting candles and praying for us every day.

Priests also in Cyprus were asked to say a prayer. My uncle got in touch with a monk at the Agio Oros, a monastery in Greece. We were getting a lot of moral support. I was not religious but as I said above, I welcomed anything that could have helped. You never know! I took everything with a pinch of salt. So maybe I was not an atheist but an agnostic?

⁓⁄⁓

The third time with IVF things were roughly the same as before. Even though we had been through it twice before, I still had to explain the process to Steve. He just didn't get it.

Men!

Only one thing was slightly different. This time they actually put the sperm directly in my eggs. This method is called Intra-cytoplasmic Sperm Injection (ICSI). I suppose, this method increases the chances of the eggs getting fertilized, as the sperm is injected in the egg, avoiding the risk of a weak sperm not being able to enter the egg by itself. Seven eggs fertilized. Hope and positivity was ripe. The eggs were left in the lab for two to three days and then they were transferred to my womb. We decided to have two eggs inseminated just in case one failed. I can remember joking with Steve, "That's my boy and that's my girl."

The waiting game was upon us again. This was truly the hardest part of the IVF process for me. I went for my blood test and the nurse asked me if I had any loss of blood. I had not. She smiled and I went home.

When the phone rang I was a bag of nerves. Listening intently, I could not believe what I was hearing. Not only was I pregnant, I was pregnant with twins. Tears rolled down my face. Tears of joy and tears of guilt. My poor darling Xristos. How could I be happy, when I knew he did not survive? My head was confused again. Steve took me in his arms, reassured me and together we started to move forward. We did not know at that point that there was going to be more heartache to come. The excitement period was very, very short indeed.

⌁

We were conservatively elated. Too many things went wrong before. If you thought we had a tough time you are mistaken. Apparently that was only the warm up. Now the battle for survival starts. What follows next can make or break a couple. It can easily go either way. We never expected nor were we prepared for what was coming.

My in-laws were brilliant. My mother-in-law came to stay with us; to do the housework and look after Vas, so that she would do nothing but rest. That was a big help to us, as Vas is quite close to her mother.

Days after our happy discovery of Vas being pregnant, she started having stomach pains. The jeans she was wearing ten days before, to our amazement, she could not get into them now. We went to our local doctor who told us that it was a virus and for Vas to drink plenty of water. That was wrong, as Vas's pains got worse. Vas called Mr. Artley's office who quite urgently told her to rush to the hospital immediately. The ambulance was called. I stayed with Vas while I asked my mother-in-law to stand by the front door to let the paramedics in. She was in so much pain that I did not want to leave her alone.

Ten minutes later my mother-in-law ran in, all panicky.

Apparently the ambulance pulled up in front of our house, stopped for ten seconds and then drove away, with the driver happily waving at my mother-in-law. They did not say anything to her, or had the courtesy to explain why they were leaving. Just like that, they drove away.

There was no time to phone for another ambulance and no guarantee that the next one would even show up, never mind transporting my wife to the hospital. I quickly picked Vas in my arms and gently put her in the car. Generally I am not a violent man. That day I could not be sure of that.

Vas was admitted straight away.

They took us to a private room.

         ✧

I said before that I was ready. I really was ready. I was just not ready for the ordeal that we were about to encounter. I don't think anyone is. You have to reach deep in your faith in God and do a lot of praying.

         ✧

My wife was sitting on the bed still in agonizing pain. My mother-in-law helped her get up, where to my horror of horrors I saw a wet patch where she was sitting.

Before I continue, I want to remind you about what I said before. For things I don't know, I really don't know anything about them. I am completely clueless

So, with dread in my heart I said, "Vas, your waters broke."

She looked at the wet patch on the bed and with a mixture of pain and a chuckle she told me that it was just some water she spilled earlier. Her waters could not have possibly broken.

Vas was kind to think that it was the stress of the ambulance men driving away that caused me to think that. I put my hands up high and admit that it was not. To this day, I still don't know how the female body works and deep down I have no real desire to find out.

Vas had ovarian hyper stimulation because of the drugs, with her ovaries ballooning to the size of balls. She could have died. They told us that most probably we would lose the babies. What a bloody rollercoaster! The elation of finding that Vas was pregnant with twins was short lived indeed.

This sometimes happens with IVF and it's something to be on the lookout for.

Mr. Artley came to see Vas as soon as we arrived at the hospital and maintained a constant look over her. If Vas had not gotten in touch with his office, to be told to come to the hospital straight away and continued listening to our doctor, I dread to think what the final outcome would have been.

～✑～

Ovarian hyper stimulation does sometimes happens because of IVF. It is dangerous and I urge any woman getting pregnant through IVF, when you see these symptoms to get checked straight away. It is better to err on the side of caution.

Disturbing your doctor or the hospital is a small price to pay when your life or your baby's life can be in danger. IVF can be a magical thing when it works, but it comes with certain risks which you have to be aware of. Our doctor was wrong. I shall be eternally grateful to Mr. Artley.

Steve was spitting feathers. He was furious with the ambulance crew. Normally he is quite easy-going. He really lost it that day. I don't blame him.

Nevertheless, I asked him not to pursue it. The babies were okay, which was all that mattered. Knowing him, he is like a dog with the bone, as tenacious as a bulldog. He was so angry, that he would have pursued it until the day he died, if that was the amount of time needed. It was an aggravation that we did not need in our lives.

The following day I wrote to the chief executive of the ambulance service voicing my complaint at the negligence and incompetence of his staff and my intention to sue. A few days later I received a letter from him stating that what really happened, was that they received a more urgent case and they had to divert the ambulance to that case. He sent his apologies and assured me that they would update their controls so that something like this would not happen again. He also offered to have a meeting at a place of convenience to me so that we would resolve this matter amicably. I replied that a service that deals in life and death on a daily basis should have already had in place controls for such eventuality where one of the controllers called the patient informing him of the situation and giving him a choice of either waiting for the next available ambulance or make his own way to the hospital. It was just shameful.

I did not take him up on the meeting as I was not sure I would have been courteous and I took him on his word that an occurrence like ours would not be repeated. From my perspective I had more pressing matters to attend to. To tell you the truth I would have chased them through the courts forever. I was that angry. I just wanted to focus my anger and hate on someone. They were perfect for it. The fact that Vas asked me to drop it though, put a stop to it. I was not too happy about it, but there you go!

You have to understand something about me here. With the exception of Vas, this ordeal had made me distant to everyone. I had that angry aura about me, that family and friends were avoiding me, as I was snappy with them. From being a placid and docile person, I turned into the kind of person I always try to avoid to be around. I was quick tempered, critical and confrontational.

They dealt with the ovarian hyper stimulation and after a further scan we confirmed that Vas was still pregnant. It was a close call for both Vas and the babies.

Our life from then on, was for Vas to be at home for two days and then three days at the hospital. This went on continuously for the next four months.

I remember when my sisters got pregnant they went through their months of pregnancy and then they gave birth; as simple as that.

When Vas fell pregnant with Xristos the first time, it was easier; this was a different pregnancy altogether.

It was a cocktail of stabs in the heart. When she had a break from the pains, Vas had to be rushed to hospital because she was bleeding. We thought that we would have lost the babies. The bleeding did not happen once. It happened lots of times and every time my heart would tighten, thinking that we were lucky the previous times and that this time we would lose the babies. Imagine your wife waking you up in the middle of the night telling you she was bleeding. Not once, but many times. You see, after so many scares, defeatism is knocked into you. Imagine facing the scares of the bleeding and then the euphoria when it stopped and then with our heart in our mouths waiting to find out if Vas was still pregnant. It was a constant barrage of scares and highs. It was relentless and it took a piece of us every time it happened. In the end it breaks you, for you expect it to happen again and deep down you feel the next time will be the killer blow. You become weak and fatalism is knocked into you without you realizing it.

Her ovaries did not shrink to their normal size immediately. So, even though they were shrinking, they were doing so at a slow pace, which left Vas still in enormous pain. Pain, bleeding, pain, bleeding. Just for the fun of it, to mix things up, Vas started puking severely which entitled her with prolonged stays at the hospital.

Another big scare was when Vas got rushed to the hospital with severe pains and when Mr. Artley examined her, he thought that it was a severely twisted bowel and that there was a good chance we would lose the babies. We survived that as well.

This sequence kept changing to keep us guessing, I suppose. What joy! We could not tell which one of them would be next.

It was hard going and nerve-wracking. I would go to bed with one eye open, waiting for Vas to wake me up, telling me that she was bleeding. If the night was quiet, we had the day to get through. It was a terrible experience. Nothing was smooth. Vas's bag was always full and ready to be taken with us to the hospital. I wouldn't have blamed them, if they decided to invite us to their staff Christmas party. We got to know everyone. We were both a bag of nerves by then.

During the first pregnancy, Vas was glowing. This time, it was chipping away a chunk of our confidence, on a daily basis. Neither of us had a good night's sleep for months. My business started to suffer, as I was rarely there. This was not how we expected our pregnancy to be. There was no laughter or joy like before.

We survived all those scares and managed to have our first scan. It was brilliant. We got to see both babies. My swimmers rose to the occasion and conquered the motherland (Joke, ha ha!).

Being that the pregnancy started difficult and it did not look as if it was it was going to get better, we decided to see a specialist in Harley Street, London. His name is Professor Nicolaides and he works for the Fetal Medicine Centre. His whole attitude and demeanor was overwhelming. He radiated tranquility and reassurance. He checked Vas and the babies and told us that even though Vas fell pregnant through IVF, it was just like any other pregnancy. We should try not worry too much. That was a much needed boost. I was glad we went to see him. His calm demeanor and reassurance recharged our depleted confidence and calmed our nerves. I think if we were living near London, we would have been going to see him every week as he is a well-known specialist in his field and it gives you reassurance to be seen by someone of that level of expertise.

~⟋~

What I have told you here is the very short version of that miserable period. It was relentless! It was terrifying! So many scares and highs. It turned me into a horrible monster.

~⟋~

We had a week to ten days where Vas did not have to see the doctor or get rushed to hospital. It really felt as if we were on holiday. A whole week without scares and no visits to the hospital! Hooray!

We thought that it would do Vas a lot of good to spend a week down in Margate with her parents; to sort of change the scenery. For the first time since she fell pregnant, she was looking radiant. It would have also given a chance to my mother-in-law to sort her own house out. We drove down Sunday morning. Sunday night I drove back home, with the intention of going back the following weekend to pick them up.

It is amazing how even the simplest plan does not work out. What you hope and what you get is not necessarily the same thing.

Vas got up on Monday morning nice and steady. She was breathing the fresh sea air of Margate, thinking that everything would go back to normal and everything that would follow was nothing more than going through a normal pregnancy. I thought so as well.

~⟋~

Being pregnant, for the second time was very scary. Many things were against me from the beginning. I was in and out of hospital, every single week.

Things seemed to calm down in the July. Steve and I decided that I should go to Margate, for a change of scenery and a rest. Steve left on Sunday, to return home because of work. On Monday night, resting in bed, I found it quite difficult to get comfortable. As I turned on my side, I felt a pop inside me and then a gush. I dare not look down, but as I got close to the toilet, I took a deep breath. As I looked down, I started screaming. I was covered in blood. Mom and dad came running out of their bedroom in panic. All three of us were in a state of shock. They managed to phone the ambulance, by which time I was back in bed, trying to stop my babies from being born. It was total chaos. The ambulance came and I was taken to Margate Hospital, where I was monitored.

The bleeding subsided and the twins were safe. It was scary as I did not have Steve by my side. I also felt awful, for the fact that I put my parents through this ordeal as well. I did not want them to be haunted by what they saw.

My father-in-law called me straight away, telling me the bad news and that he would call me back as soon as he had any more news. Guilt and torment engulfed me, as I was second guessing myself. I should not have driven her all the way there. It was probably the driving that had caused it, etc…

He called me later on, telling me that the bleeding had reduced drastically and they were keeping Vas in for monitoring. I spoke to her later on. The babies were doing fine and she was feeling weak. We were on the phone every day. They decided to keep her in, as one day she would bleed heavily and then the following day the bleeding would stop or reduce.

The amount of the bleeding, the unpredictability of it and the fact that she was pregnant with twins reinforced their desire to keep her there for monitoring. For the whole week, her bleeding was like this: heavy at first, then stopped; slow and then heavy. Not a day went by that week, without her having some kind of a bleed. The only difference this time, she was without me the whole week. My father-in-law told me to stay up, as there was nothing I could do there but stand and watch. They were there with her every day, anyway. I would talk to her on the phone daily. We were both worried but we were both lying to each other that everything would be alright. What else could we say? We were scared shitless and we did not know how we were going to fare the next day or the one after that.

Gone were the plans to bring Vas home on the weekend. Instead I was only visiting as she was in no state to travel. She was bleeding the day before again. In total she stayed ten days in that hospital. On the tenth day they gave Vas an injection to help the babies' lungs develop.

I think I managed just over a week at Margate Hospital before the next big scare. Once again, whilst I was trying to get comfortable, I turned and then I felt the pop again and then the gush. I pressed the emergency button and I started screaming. The nurses ran into my room and gasped at the blood loss. I was covered in blood and so was the bed.

I had to put all my faith in them. This was totally out of my control.

I was also worried for my dad. He had some health issues a couple of years back and my being there and seeing me bleeding, I was worried that it would affect him terribly.

The following night she started losing blood heavily. The difference this time was that Vas was also contracting. The hospital in Margate was not equipped to deal with two so premature babies. The decision was taken to transfer Vas to Gillingham Maritime Hospital. It is situated about thirty miles from Margate. I received the call from my father-in-law. I hated it when I heard his voice on the phone by then. Every damn call from him was bad news. He could not help it, but I could not help it either.

There they had a newly set up unit that dealt specifically with premature babies. I guess that was the best place for Vas and the babies as even our local hospital would not have been able to cope. She was taken straight to the delivery room, as she was contracting and they thought she was about to give birth. Thankfully the contractions stopped. After a while with no sign of them starting again, she was transferred to the maternity ward.

Early Sunday morning I drove to Gillingham to see my wife. She was on a drip of some liquid of some kind and she was also having blood transfusions at regular intervals. She wasn't looking too good but she had a smile on her face. She tried to reassure me that things were not dangerous, but I saw through it. Bless her. From the beginning, her whole pregnancy was a nightmare. I could see that she was fearful.

What women should see out of this is that we become spectators. Vas was carrying the babies, having blood transfusions, living with the scare twenty-four hours a day. She did what the doctors told her. She was carrying the weight of our family all by herself. I, on the other hand felt impotent. I could not do anything apart from watching and offering empty bloody words of encouragement. My role as a protector for my family had been taken away from me and I was full of anger and frustration.

After I had a chat with the doctor, I asked everyone to leave, including my in-laws. Vas and I had to talk.

She was shaken to the core by this and she was scared to death with worry about our twins. For Vas it was like reliving the end part of her first pregnancy. She was determined to hold out for as long as possible, so as to give our twins a fighting chance of survival. For her, it was make or break time. Either the twins would come out to join us alive, or if not

I am sure Vas would have been a broken woman. She would have lost her sanity. I am not exaggerating here!

I knew there and then, there would have been no more IVF attempts for us or trying to fall pregnant. It was just too much. We were at the crossroads of our lives and neither turn looked very promising.

We had a private half hour where we talked candidly about our situation. It was emotional and quite helpful. Even at that stage I was amazed at the depth of Vas's desire to become a mother. Our situation sucked…Our lives sucked…Our future sucked…

We had reached the stage that having a Caesarian was imminent if the bleeding continued. However for every day that Vas managed to hang on, it would have given the babies a greater chance of survival. Every day was a blessing. She was only five months into her pregnancy. I was dreading it. Even if she held out for a month it would still be too early for the babies.

On Monday I was back home running the business. On Tuesday a supplier came in the shop and after he brought everything in, he decided to tell me that he had an old Porsche 928(car) and that he told his two daughters that the first one who gave him a grandson (not a grandchild) would get the car. (What an idiot!) I did not flinch. I told him to pick everything up and that I did not need the delivery, I had already ordered. He tried to reason with me. I glared at him with that crazy look. He left and to this day I have never dealt with his company. I had changed without even realizing it. I was becoming an antisocial monster!

In the meantime back in Gillingham the bleeding lessened drastically and there was talk of discharging Vas at the end of the week as she was now having minor bleeds. When I talked to her on the phone, we were both jubilant. We could scratch that down as one more scare among the plethora of others we had been through. It was a relief, as they would have been born way too early at five and a half months.

Those months were so hard. It was a non-stop sequence of highs and scares. Little by little it breaks you, without you realizing it. It sucks the life out you and there is not a damned thing you can do about it. The only thing you hope is that you remain strong enough to survive it and if you are lucky to see it through to the end.

It was Friday evening. Almost three weeks since I first brought Vas down to Margate.

There was a heat-wave. I was ratty and uncomfortable. I told mom I was fine and asked her to go home. I did not feel like having company. I was hot and bothered and it was getting late. She had to drive home.

I took myself to the toilet. I saw that there was blood, but not a lot. It was not bright red. It was a darker color and thicker. It was just different.

I thought I should inform the nurses. I was not worried as that was nothing compared to my previous blood losses. I expected them to come and tell me, "Don't worry, love, it is nothing to worry about". Instead, the nurse that came in said, "Oh my God. I need to get you in a wheelchair and take you to the labor ward".

The attending doctor, a junior, had an argument with her. He reckoned she overreacted. Bless her, she stuck to her guns and would not let me leave the labor ward. She was an experienced nurse with more experience in this than him. She thought that I should have had a Caesarean. He dismissed the idea and relented only in keeping me there.

A couple of hours later I started bleeding heavily but this time, they were pulling large pieces of clotted blood away from my person.

True to his form, I received the dreaded call from my father-in-law again. Vas was losing so much blood, that the transfusions could not keep up. It was as if someone left the tap open. Apparently they were now considering an emergency Caesarean because if the situation continued it was both dangerous for her and the babies. She was booked in the early hours of the morning. Unless the bleeding stopped, they would operate.

I gave the keys to a member of staff and was down there within two hours and fifteen minutes. I don't remember much of the drive. I was driving at dangerously high speeds, like a lunatic. As soon as my mother-in-law got home, she had to turn back with my father in law to be at Vas's side.

When I reached there, I was shocked. A nurse was doing something behind Vas's back. I reached over to give her a hug and all I heard was a scream from my mother-in-law, "No!" I stopped and looked at her questioningly. They were giving Vas an epidural. It is such a delicate procedure that any sudden movement on her part, could have had catastrophic consequences. Vas was beside herself. The decision was made that a Caesarian had to be performed as soon as possible, according to the doctor. She was losing so much blood that the blood transfusions could not keep up. Her life was in danger as well as the twins. She tried to smile at me as soon as the nurse finished, but instead she burst into tears.

The monitor was attached to her and I could hear the twins' heartbeats. It sounded like horses galloping.

"Why could I not hold out a bit longer? It is too soon. The twins will have no chance. What can we do?" she said in between the tears and sobs.

What could I say to that?

I cuddled her and told her that the extra days she managed to hold out would hopefully make all the difference. Did I believe it? Of course not; it was too bloody soon.

Then she voiced the unthinkable "What if I refuse to have it? I may be able to hold out for maybe a week or two. With God's help the twins might have a better chance."

How could she say that, when she was deathly white and having continuous blood transfusions? "Don't worry about me" she said. I could not believe what I was hearing. She expected me to support her on such a thing.

Even though Vas knew that I was not religious, I would still go with her to church on Sunday. I believe that everybody is free and welcomed to believe anything they want, as long as they don't try to force their beliefs onto others. Live and let live. However, that was not the time or the place for a religious debate or any kind of debate. To allow it to turn into a debate would have implied there was even the tiniest chance that I could have been persuaded to agree.

That was real life. Vas could have believed as much as she wanted for all I cared. I would be damned if I was going to let her turn me in to a widower based on some delusion that her God existed and was righteous.

We wanted to start our family and get to experience the joys of raising and guiding our children. I was fine with that. We had not even started yet and Vas was talking about endangering her life. I was not okay with that. It was probably nature's way of telling us to give it up. We were probably never meant to be parents. There was still the option of adoption or even getting a dog! There was no option in letting Vas endanger her life. What started like a dream was quickly turning into a nightmare.

This small built-woman, this giant; was willing to sacrifice herself to give our babies a fighting chance. I was not so willing, nor did I share her belief in God. The whole situation was unbelievably absurd. Three days ago we were jubilant as the bleeding reduced drastically and now we were dealing with life and death. The quick changes in fortunes and emotions were overpowering and unsettling. However this time Vas's life was in danger.

Her selflessness and desire to protect the twins would have really killed her. I did not know whether to kiss her or slap her. That is why I married her. That is why there is hope I could become a better person. There was no bloody way I was going to let her risk her life though. If the outcome of the pregnancy was bad by me stopping her, she could have hated me in later years. I was willing to live with that. At that moment in time I felt it was the right thing to do. I was selfish. I just wanted to get my wife back in one piece.

I looked Vas in the eyes and told her that she had done well to carry the babies that far. The extra few days she gave them would hopefully make all the difference. I did not really believe what I was saying. I was hoping it was true. It was just too early. I just had to convince her of that. I firmly told her that since the doctor felt that she had to have a Caesarian, then she had to do it. I knew and appreciated her longing to be a mother. I wanted to be a father as well. But after seeing how dire our situation was, enough was enough. We had to follow the medical advice and hope for the best. My lioness relented. Even if she did not, I would have overruled her. I was a bag of nerves and I did not want to take any more risks.

Our predicament was dire and I felt I was drowning. Vas's statement for me, was what broke the camel's back. I just wished we were back home and still trying to fall pregnant the normal way. I wanted us to be anywhere but there.

Where she was bleeding, to my horror, it was not just blood gushing out. I saw the nurse pull a massive blood clot out of her. I was shocked. My father-in-law told me that that was not the first one.

Without looking at her, I nodded to the doctor to go ahead and prepare everything. I was not prepared to give her a chance to voice her opinion. It really was not a debate any more. I squeezed her hand a little hard, to let her know that I was not in the mood to hear anything.

Vas was distraught. It was just too bloody soon. She was only five and a half months pregnant. All three were in danger as she continued to lose so much blood. There was just no end to this nightmare ride. I held her hand gently this time and with the smile I told her again, that the extra days she gave them would make all the difference. I cannot remember how many times I repeated that untrue statement in such a short time. She gave me a sad smile and nodded. She could not speak. But her eyes were shedding tears and at the same time, screaming out about how scared and worried she was. I squeezed her hand and patted her on her shoulder.

There was nothing else to be said. What was going to happen was out of our control. I was hoping that Vas would come out of this without any damage. She had lost so much blood. I was hoping that the hospital was equipped with expertise and advanced medical equipment to perform a miracle on our behalf. Everything depended on them now. Vas was going to be in the thick of it, while my only job was to stand next to her and watch. I don't know if it was the feeling of uselessness and loss of control. Panic set in me. I felt that Vas's trip to the operating room was opening the door to Hell. I just had that premonition that we were both going to our doom. I did not want us to take that trip. Not now. Not yet.

I was embarrassed about some nurse knowing I masturbated. Here was Vas having continuous blood transfusions, having no control over her body and putting herself in mortal danger in order to try to bring to this world our two babies. Carrying the weight of our family all by herself. Mothers are our lioness. It is as simple as that.

How we envisioned our pregnancy to be and how it turned out to be could not have been more different. Once again what we got was a dose of nightmares which as wannabe future parents were unprepared and inexperienced to deal with. We just wanted to be parents. That's all. We thought it was going to be simple. It was Hell. There was nothing apart from worry and despair.

We had to face our destiny. We were dealt some shitty cards and the game was rigged against us. Damn her God and damn this fucking world! What had we done that was so bad, that we had to suffer like this?

Time waits for no man. The time for words was over as she was whisked to the operating room. I wished I could stop time and delay this trip. I wished Vas was still in her room and nurturing our babies in her belly for another three and a half months. I wished…

Chapter 9

Giving Birth

The doors to the operating room swung open and we were inside. Everyone was busy in there with their own tasks. I was standing next to Vas holding her hand. The consultant came over with two junior doctors who were going to assist him. It was such a weird experience. As they were putting some kind of liquid on Vas's belly, where they were going to cut her, the consultant was actually being quite abrupt towards one of the junior doctors. I remember looking at my wife to see if she noticed this juncture and she gave me a knowing look. We made no comment. Here we were on the brink of the abyss and they couldn't sort their differences in private. The whole situation was ludicrous.

When I knew I was going for the Caesarean section, I wanted to be knocked out. I did not want to live-through the experience conscious; aware. It was just too soon. It was not an option though. It was a surreal experience. Physically I was not in pain. Mentally I was being tortured.

There was a lot of tugging, pulling and rushing around by the attending doctors.

A doctor approached me with some forms to sign. Apparently we had two choices regarding breathing methods; that could be given to premature babies. One was the conventional ventilator (CV) and the second was a new one, the High Frequency Oscillatory Ventilation (HFOV). How do you decide which method to give to whom? Why couldn't they both have the same method? Why did they give me an option? What if my decision was to condemn one or both of my babies to death? How did they expect me to decide, with my wife bleeding and me not in the right frame of mind? Plus, I had no idea about breathing methods.

What was my decision? I told the doctor that the first baby out of Vas's belly was to have the CV and the second to have the HFOV—in those seconds I decided the fates of both our unborn children.

Obviously I did not know if Andrea was going to come out first or Petros. I thought that this way was fair on both of them and if I made the wrong decision and condemned one of them through my ignorance, I had the rest of my life to live with the guilt, torment and regret.

That was a brilliant continuation of the shitty things that occurred that day.

I think I speak for most men, in that we always want a son. We can play football and catch with him and have beers when he grows up. The son is also the continuation of the surname, the patriarchal condition placed in all our minds. Here is where I stand on this point now. Had we not known the sex of the babies, the response I would have given was, as long as my wife and babies come out of it healthy, I don't care about the sex of the babies.

I was standing right by Vas's side as they were cutting her. You hear of people going in for surgery and they sometimes proudly show you their scars. But to actually see your wife getting cut right in front of your eyes and to actually see inside her body is weird. You see her at her most vulnerable. If this does not bring you closer together, I don't know what does.

This woman, like the majority of women, was willing to do anything and face any danger in order to have her babies. Seeing her lying on the bed with her belly cut open and in fear for the safety of the babies and not herself, I made a promise to myself that I should be a better husband. She deserved this, the same as every other mother on this planet.

My heart was in my mouth. The next few minutes would be pivotal to the course our lives would take from then on. At that very minute all scenarios did not look promising. We really needed a miracle; from God according to Vas and through the advance of medicine and science according to me.

They were ready to take the babies out. I could see the consultant put his hands in Vas's belly, pulling the first baby out and handing the baby to the nurse. She very quickly took the baby to a doctor, whom I did not realize was there; apparently because the babies were so premature they had a doctor on the left side of the room waiting.

I heard the nurse say the baby was a girl.

That was Andrea. Her skin looked very dark. I was expecting to hear Andrea cry or move; deadly silence amongst the chaos of the operating room—but my ears were listening for that one little whimper of life from her. There was no movement. I got very worried and moved closer. The doctor tried to revive her while checking her vitals. It did not last long. "It's no use. She is dead", said the doctor. Just like that my daughter was pronounced dead. All my worries about how early the babies were coming out materialized there and then. They were just too bloody early. If Vas's God existed, where was he when you needed him the most? Did he take a day off? How much crap can a couple take before they break down? For I was close to the abyss now, and when a man stares too long into that abyss…that abyss stares back into him.

I immediately went back to my wife and told her. There was no room for sugarcoating the truth here. With Andrea dead, it was only a matter of moments before we found out whether Petros was alive or not. The look of pain in her eyes broke my heart. There she was, lying on her back with her belly cut open and I was telling her that our daughter was dead. She was as helpless as I was. Dread overtook me. We were going to be destroyed as a family. If Andrea came out dead, what chance did Petros have? I was there in the room but at the same time I wasn't.

When Steve told me that Andrea had died, I felt numb. My little girl was gone forever. I was not going to take her shopping, comb her hair, buy her clothes, love her and spoil her. I was totally destroyed. With Andrea gone, what chance did Petros have? My babies!

Petros was now taken out of Vas and rushed to the doctor. Again I heard no crying nor seen any movement. His skin was the same color as Andrea's. Desperation and panic set in. I just knew that Petros was dead as well. The doctor had the same concerned look on his face. I asked him what was wrong. In between trying to revive Petros, he told me that from the time they brought him there, he had not taken a single breath. He continued and then suddenly he stopped.

"It's no use." The doctor told me, "There has not been a heartbeat or any oxygen to his brain. Even if by some miracle he gets a heartbeat, his brain has been starved of oxygen for so long that he will be brain dead. It is better if we let him go."

Words cannot describe my feelings, so I will not try. I will only drag you to a dark place where monsters live and from where there is no return. No human being should go through that despair.

I knew that I just could not go over to my wife and tell her that Petros was dead as well. So much misery and hopelessness! I could not tell her that she would be going home without any of her babies. That would have mentally destroyed her. She was in a fragile state already. I knew that going over with the news would have sent her over the edge into the abyss. To want to be a mother so much, fall pregnant with two babies and end up going home without any of them was something that I definitely knew would have driven her insane. I knew my wife and I knew that I would have lost her as well.

I looked him straight in the eyes and pleaded, "Please don't stop. I have already told my wife that our baby girl died. I can't go back and tell her our baby boy is dead as well. I just can't."

He was adamant, "It is pointless...It has been ten minutes now."

We had embarked on this journey to become a family. Whether I was still going to have a family depended on what actions this stranger took in the next several seconds. He quite literally held my future in his hands.

Full of despair and with tears in my eyes I told him, "If you stop, you are not just killing my son, but also my wife. She will not be able to survive this. She will not be able to go home without at least one baby. Please, continue trying. Please!"

I could tell that he disagreed with me, but he continued to try to revive Petros nonetheless.

However strong a person I was, I knew I just could not face Vas and tell her that Petros was dead as well. So much misery, death and despair!

Consequently I decided to stay there with the doctor until the end. I had nowhere else in the world to go to. If you were going to stab me at that time; no blood would have come out of me. I was just frozen with panic as I felt that my whole life was crumbling around me.

There was just no movement or reaction from Petros. Inside me, I was I was egging him to cry. To do something, that would show he was alive. To somehow link with me and tell me, "Help me dad. Don't give up on me. Don't let them…" There was nothing…Nothing at all! As quiet as a graveyard! How appropriate, as I was surrounded by death. My son was lifeless…His skin was still very dark like Andrea's and I heard no cry nor did I see any movement. Dread was overpowering me. Dark, menacing clouds were hovering on top of me. In a matter of seconds my family, my unit and my life was going to crumble to nothingness. No babies…No wife…Nothing…No dreams…Just nightmares and regrets…Just anger and hate…I felt so alone…

Suddenly without any warning, the doctor handed Petros to the nurse and told her to quickly put him in the incubator and take him to the Neo Natal High Dependency Unit. I did not hear Petros cry or see him open his eyes. I did not even see his chest move. I was confused. Was he dead or alive?

The doctor turned to me, and said, "This is a long shot. Don't get your hopes up. Remember; he might not even survive the trip to Neo Natal. He might not even stay alive within the next hour." He set off to follow the nurse and stopped. "I am not trying to scare you" he said, "Even if he survives this, the fact that no oxygen went to his brain for so long, the chances are that he will not be functional but instead be like a vegetable". He gave me a sad smile and hurriedly went the same way, the nurse left with my son.

There I was, left standing by myself like a lemon, unable to get my brain to function. I wanted to move but my body was not responding. I remember I took a massive deep breath and shook my head. That seemed to have done the trick. I still did not know whether Petros was alive or dead.

Shaky and unsteady on my feet I went over to Vas. It seemed I was taking forever to cover such a short distance. That was the empty shell of the strong man that I was, going over to my wife. Those last few minutes sucked the life out me. I just did not know what was happening. I think my subconscious was hoping that by taking longer to reach my wife, someone would burst in the room cheering that Petros was fine and well. No one burst in. I finally reached Vas. Still shaking I told her, "They have taken Petros to Neo Natal. We just have to wait and see what happens." I did not tell her that he did not have a heartbeat or that he not taken a breath for ten minutes. It was pointless. That would have crushed her. I held her hand for reassurance as much for her as for me. I smiled for I did not want her to see the fear and despair on my face. The consultant was in the process of stitching Vas's caesarean. All this started about 6:30am in the morning September the fourth—Now it was 7:10am.

Vas saw through my false smile and started crying. I squeezed her hand. I don't know how much longer we stayed in the operating theatre or when we got back to the room. It was as if there was no one around me apart from Vas. The world was such a lonely place. I was sure Petros was not going to survive. I wanted the door to our room to be nailed shut so that no one could come in and give us the dreaded news that I expected to happen. I just knew the first doctor or nurse that came through the door would deliver the news that Petros did not make it. After going through the experience of losing Xristos and the new grief of losing Andrea that hadn't even begun to sink in yet, losing Petros would have been the final nail in the coffin lid.

You will notice that Vas did not share a lot about this time of our lives. It is still daunting for her and has no wish to relive it. She is still scarred and I don't think there will be a time when she will feel ready to talk about it. I don't blame her. She is a gentle person who, how she expected life to be and how it turned out for her, were two extremely different stories. She had just too many scares that shook her to the core. In the present of 2015, we sometimes talk about this period between us in private. Her eyes will fill up. If she wishes to continue, I carry on with the conversation. If she feels she has to stop, it's okay with me. The healing process is long and we are in no hurry. She has been scarred and she knows if she is ready or not. I am patient and I shall wait. There is no pressure for Vas to relive it.

If only this was the end of our troubles. If only we could let out a sigh of relief and been allowed to have a go at rebuilding our lives and regrouping.

No such luck.

That would have been too easy.

Our romantic dream of becoming parents had turned into a nightmare. It all seemed so easy before we started. Even after she fell pregnant we thought we might get lucky and have a normal pregnancy! Giving birth was a nightmare. Now we had to deal with the consequences of those results. Every bad decision you make will eventually come to bite you on the ass.

I hoped I did not make too many of them.

Previously, when I found out that I was pregnant, with a boy and a girl, I thought, "Finally, I have got my perfect little family. I am going to give it my all and I shall not want anything else in my life, ever."

Chapter 10

Trials & Tributions

B eing that Petros came out second, he was given the HFOV ventilator. By Petros being on that ventilator he was by default part of the United Kingdom Oscillation Study (UKOS).

What is HFOV and UKOS?

The Study / UKOS. **ukos**.wordpress.com/the-study/

Initial study (1998-2001) Babies were recruited to the initial **UKOS** study...Both types of **ventilation** were routinely used in neonatal units when **UKOS** started.

The Study {*Initial study (1998-2001)}** Babies were recruited to the initial UKOS study between 1998 and 2001. They were recruited from 22 hospitals in the UK, and one in each of Ireland, Australia and Singapore. Babies could enter the study if they were born between 23 weeks and 28 weeks, had no congenital abnormalities, and required help with their breathing. 797 babies were recruited to the study.

At birth, infants were randomised to be ventilated (to help their breathing) using High Frequency Oscillatory Ventilation (HFOV) or Conventional Ventilation (CV). Both types of ventilation were routinely used in neonatal units when UKOS started.

Babies were assessed extensively while in hospital and then re-assessed at age six months, one year and two years. None of these assessments uncovered any clear differences between the two ways of ventilating the children.

It's a fast method of pushing air into the lungs. It made Petros look as if he was shaking.

It did not even cross my mind at the time that Petros was on the HFOV ventilator or how important that was. Not for at least a month. Small details like this are forgotten in the face of calamity. It was such an important detail though.

Petros survived the trip to Neo Natal and the next hour.

Vas was transferred back to the maternity ward. She was in a lot of pain. She was in agony! She could not sleep and kept feeling sick. She was given gas and air to relieve the pain, which made her feel more nauseous. Unbeknownst to me at the time, that was the second series of constant scares which would shake me to the core and try to turn me into a person that I would normally avoid.

"Beware that, when fighting monsters, you yourself do not become a monster…for when you gaze long into the abyss, the abyss gazes also into you." This quote by Friedrich Nietzsche does not just apply to the wars men fight with each other, or our own demons; it also applies to a person battling against the very world itself…and in our case the battle to bring life into it.

When Vas was up to it, we walked very slowly down to Neo Natal to see Petros. His eyelids had not opened yet. They were not fully formed.

He also had no nipples. He was so tiny. It was so stupid of me. I was actually alarmed by the fact that he had no nipples. Not that he was hanging by a thread, but that he had no nipples. Go figure!

He had tubes coming out of every part of his body. The damn alarms kept going off with the tireless nurses running to him and trying to sort him out.

His lungs were not fully formed and he could not breathe on his own. Nothing was fully formed as he only weighed less than a bag of sugar.

When we first saw him we despaired. He was so little and fragile that I was so sure he was not going to survive this ordeal, when a fully formed ten pound baby died the other day. What chance did my son have?

When Petros was born, he weighed a mere 685 grams. He was the tiniest baby I had ever seen in my life. How was this small baby expected to survive when nothing on him was fully formed? Every step of our journey was filled with worry. Why could we not catch a lucky break? Why couldn't we be given the chance to smile? It had been such a long time.

In the pictures Petros looks bigger than he actually was. I think I could have held him in the palm of my hand.

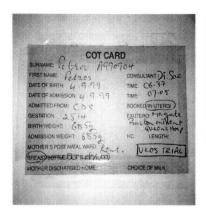
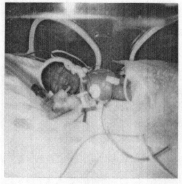

We had to sterilize our hands before we entered Neo Natal. Being that all babies were in some kind of monitoring or another, the last thing anyone wanted was for a visitor to spread germs on the already fragile babies. There was a hole in the incubator where you could put your hand in for physical contact. We dare not do that. So many tubes! He looked like an alien! What worried me the most was this; there was actually no sign of life. The only movement was his chest as it was being forcefully pushed by the ventilator. That movement was done for him and not by him. Other than that, he just laid there looking lifeless. Even the slightest hope we had was taken away from us as soon as we saw this. He was such a little thing. In the pictures his skin looks pink. I think it was more the flash of the camera than anything else. His skin was hanging from his little bones as he had no muscles. It looked as if it was empty. How can a body fill up and develop with a start like this?

The warnings of the doctor came to haunt me, "He may be brain damaged and a vegetable…" but I brushed them away. Now was not the time. It was not as if we had any other option; and it may have been selfish of me to want Petros to survive, however slim a chance he had. The thing was, I was thinking of my wife. Even though Petros was in there fighting against astronomical odds, this very action gave Vas courage and hope. It kept her from going over into her own personal abyss for the time being. I was hoping that Petros would live to fight another minute, another hour and another day. For the time being my life was governed by those precious minutes, hours. It was what kept me going as well. Moments, that's all we get in this life and standing watching those moments grow into minutes then hours was all I could hope for at that time.

I didn't want to hear the famous lines from the movie 'Blade Runner' in my mind, "All these moments will be lost in time forever, like tears in the rain." I would have gone insane. I just wanted him to fight for his life, to win his battle against becoming just a tear in the rain. I wanted him to survive so I could take him home and tell him I was his dad and Vas was his mom. He was the thread that kept Vas together. He was the thread that kept us all going. It was such a fragile thread.

During our first visit the alarm monitors must have gone off twenty times. The tireless nurses were always there trying to sort him out.

His hands and feet had two or three needles each. Some of them were connected to the monitors, while the others were connected to tubes.

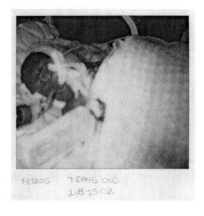

After the operation, my body did not feel right. I was in a lot of pain and could not stand up straight. A walk of five minutes took me half an hour. My body was failing me.

I was instructed by the doctors to start walking as soon as possible. The walk to Neo Natal was long and painful. As soon as I saw my baby, I just broke down. He was covered in wires and looked in pain. I felt awful. I did not want my baby to suffer.

That was my job.

The consultant wanted to talk to us and led us in his room. I must have looked terrible. In fact I was close to passing out. Needless to say, the trip back to the ward was in a wheelchair.

Steve never told me until a few months later about Petros' lack of breathing and heartbeat during the first few minutes of his life and his begging of the doctor not to give up on him. I am glad I did not know at the time.

I do remember the day after giving birth to Petros; a doctor telling me that he would not survive. My answer to him, was, "My son has survived one day. If he can survive one day, then he can pull through." I think he was quite shocked with my reply. I was not going to give up on Petros. I could not. My life and sanity depended on it.

Vas was still in pain and being sick. She seemed to be getting worse. Some nurses felt that she should not have been transferred back to the ward as it was extra work for them. The doctor insisted that she should stay.

The following night they gave her sleeping tablets, as she could not sleep because of the constant pain. She had a needle in her hand for the drip. An hour later she started hallucinating. Even though we were alone in the room and we had not seen anyone for hours, she kept telling me that members of my family, from Cyprus, were waiting outside and that I should let them in. At one stage, she got up, disconnected the drip and started talking gibberish. Due to the fact that the needle was still in her hand, she started bleeding. There she was, standing, bleeding and making no sense. It was such a heartbreaking thing to witness. I thought that I was losing my wife. I thought that she was losing her mind, after the ordeal of the caesarean and seeing Petros in the Neo Natal Unit. I called a nurse, who reconnected the drip, while I was holding Vas in a tight embrace. We stayed like that for hours, until she eventually fell asleep. I stayed awake the whole night. A full box of sleeping tablets would not have been able to knock me to sleep. I was worried that if I fell asleep and she woke up, she could have disconnected the drip again and probably bled to death without any of us knowing.

In the morning when she woke up, she was alert and making sense. We later found out that she was allergic to sleeping tablets. It was the tablets that made her hallucinate. When their effects worn off and she woke up the next morning, she remembered what happened. She tried to apologize about what happened.

I stopped her. There was no need.

The next day the nurse that whisked Vas urgently to the labor ward came in. She told Vas that she should file a complaint against that doctor as she should have had the Caesarean straight away. Vas did not want to. She felt that with Petros' life hanging in the balance, she could not and did not want to deal with that, at that point in time.

Then it all clicked, for me. The junior doctor, who was being told off by the consultant, was the one that dismissed the nurse as being too panicky. Apparently, after seeing Vas's condition, unknown to us, the consultant was having a go at him, for delaying Vas's Caesarean. Normally I would have been on the war path, demanding and expecting heads to roll. Now was not the time. Vas did not want to, anyway.

⌒⌒

Now trying to get across, to certain powers that I was not well, was another challenge; I was literally banging my head against the wall. They thought it was depression and I had to convince them that it was not. They thought I was imagining the pain.

In the meantime, I was expressing my milk for my baby. One time whilst expressing, a doctor came in and told me that Petros was not going to make it through the night. I stayed by his side, crying and trying to focus on his little face, but could not see it, for all the tears. A lovely lady, whose baby was next to Petros' incubator, took me aside and hugged me tight.

"He is going to be okay" she said, "They said the same thing to me as well, last week".

As the week progressed, I could not express milk any more. My body was so weak. I was vomiting by now, up to thirty times a day. I was hungry and thirsty, but I could not keep anything down. I was not sleeping and not taken seriously either.

I had to get out of there. I remember telling Steve "If I don't leave now, I shall end up being carried out in a coffin". I had lost so much weight in a matter of days. The pain was unbearable and I actually felt that I started to go insane.

When we told the staff that I was leaving, their reply was, "Well, you do look a lot better, dear." I could not believe what I was hearing.

⁓⁓

Vas overheard one of the nurses complaining that she was creating extra work for them. During those first days, she could not get out of bed to visit Petros because of the intense pain. She was frustrated that the pain was explained as post-natal depression. She told me that she wanted to be discharged. I should have overruled her, for she was still in pain and still puking. I was the clear headed one and I dropped the ball again!

We decided that she should stay at her parent's house and drive the daily thirty mile trip to Gillingham.

⁓⁓

On our way to my parent's house, we did the obligatory stops for my sick breaks along the way.

That night was an extremely long night. I must have had ten long hot baths, trying to numb the pain. The carpets and towels were soaked.

The next morning, mom phoned the doctor for an emergency appointment. Waiting for the time to pass was like watching paint dry.

I was rocking back and forth like a crazy woman, in absolute agony. I was filling sick bowls three, four and five at a time, full of green/black bile.

The doctor took one look at me and could not believe what he was seeing. I was immediately admitted to the hospital.

The nurses were lovely and very sympathetic towards me. I was assessed and put on strong medication straight away. The problem was though, I was still being sick. The medication took the pain away, but not the sickness. I was still losing weight and looking even rougher.

Vas was admitted to the Queen Elizabeth the Queen Mother Hospital in Margate. She could not eat. Whatever she put in her mouth she would puke it out soon after. She continued puking even though she was not eating. The doctors were baffled. She was wasting away. They put a drip in her, so that she would not dehydrate. The puking continued with a vengeance. I was sleeping on the floor by her bed. I would spend time with her and then I would drive to the other hospital where my son was fighting for his life as well.

That was when I began to question and hate God. What kind of a just God leaves someone's wife fighting for her life in one hospital and his son in another? This was supposed to be the happiest period of our life. This was supposed to be our miracle. Instead it became my living nightmare. There I was in the middle of it, being a mere spectator, unable to do anything to help my family. It just looked to me that if there was a God, he got his kicks from people's despair and misery. For my despair and misery was mounting by the minute. I saw no beauty in the world but just utter black gloom. Life and the world was a gray slate with me riveted to the center unable to see beyond my own horrors.

Unless I wanted to call the hospital where Petros was, I refused to accept any calls. The only person I would call was my mother in Cyprus who was beside herself with worry.

There is a small church near our family house and I think my mom was operating it all by herself. She was holding to her religious beliefs as well. I was surrounded by people who thought a prayer would make everything alright, not realizing that life sucked and that their religion was just a myth. She was going twice a day to light candles and say a prayer for Vas and Petros. I would give her a quick update and tell her to tell the rest of our immediate family, as I did not want anyone else calling me.

I was full of hate and anger and receiving words of support was not important or had any need for. Words were useless as it was not me who was suffering. Words would not make Vas or Petros get any better. Pretty soon friends and family stopped calling as they realized I was not in a talking mood. On reflection I should have been more understanding and courteous about their feelings as they were genuinely concerned and it could have helped talking about it to someone else. I just could not give a flying monkey about anyone else's feelings. My family was trapped in gray-quicksand and quickly going under and I was not in a talking mood. Gritting my jaw, watching all this unfold around me was Hell—if there is such a place—and I was in it.

Every morning when I awoke, I would check that Vas was still with me in this world. By now she had lost so much weight that she was a shadow of her former self. She was actually thinner than she was before she fell pregnant. She weighed roughly about seven and a half stones before she fell pregnant. She is not big built.

All this in the space of a few weeks; she had black rings around her eyes and she looked deathly pale. When I confirmed that she was still somehow okay, I would place a call to the other hospital to ensure my son had also survived the night. I would spend some time with Vas and then I would drive to the other hospital. There I would see my dear son looking so small and weak, that it would drive me near crazy. How can this tiny baby with literally just skin hanging from his tiny bones and full of tubes, survive? His eyelids had not opened yet. When he was in pain there was no sound coming out of him. He looked so fragile. The only movement I could see was the one the ventilator forced on him. It was a heartbreaking sight to see.

While I was standing there looking at him feeling overwhelmed by despair, I would sometimes smile, thinking it was just a bloody nightmare and I would soon wake up. Well, I never awoke because I wasn't bloody sleeping. I was still standing there and my son was still trying to survive the next moment. The smile was no longer on my face. It was replaced by a heavy frown. I would then question the nurse on duty as to how Petros was progressing. Progressing was the wrong word. Surviving was more appropriate. For, every time they thought that he was somehow stabilizing he would take two steps back. Those damn monitors kept going off. I would hear them in my sleep! Then I would jolt myself awake and realize that I was just terror-dreaming them.

When I returned, I would tell Vas how our son was still fighting and getting stronger. That was a lie, but she had to hear some good news to boost her confidence. She just had to hang in there. They both had to because there was nothing I could do to make them get better.

You only had to spend five minutes in my shoes to realize my despair. My bloody life was falling apart and there was not a damn thing I could do. I was living it twenty-four hours a day and with every subsequent day my life got worse instead of better. I had enough hate and anger to fill an ocean. My business was steadily going down as I was never there. Everything was falling apart!

Vas's condition deteriorated dramatically. She hadn't eaten in weeks but she continued puking. I lost faith in the doctors. Well, not just the doctors but in everything.

I wanted to take Vas away to another hospital for a second opinion. I was told that if she left, they would not re-admit her. There were thoughts flying around that she was suffering from severe post-natal depression and she obviously did not know it. They did not know what was wrong with her, so they latched onto that, justifying their theory that it was all in Vas's head. Vas looked me in the eyes and told me quite categorically that it was wrong. She felt there was something wrong inside her.

That was good enough for me. I had just about had it with the doctors. I placed a call to the chief executive's office of the hospital and spoke to his secretary. I then made a formal complaint about the quality of treatment my wife was receiving as they did not know what was wrong with her and she was getting worse. Being that the complaint was on record, they immediately arranged a meeting with me and some specialists.

My father-in-law was with me at the meeting. He is quite an easy going person who believes in dialogue. As soon as we went in the room he introduced himself, thanking them for seeing us and then asked everybody how they were. I could not believe what I was hearing. They only reason they were there was because I made an official complaint and they were covering themselves against litigation. This was not the time or place for small talk. My family was wasting away…I whispered sharply in his ear, "Please stop!" I wanted action…I wanted results…I did not go there to be sociable. What a jerk I was. His daughter was wasting away but he was still polite. My father-in-law was that understanding and easy going that he stopped. I think if I was in his position I would not have been so gracious and understanding towards me. Well, as I said before my in-laws are great. I took point at the meeting and very succinctly told them my grievances. There was no politeness nor was there any human emotion. Just anger, hate and despair. A couple of times they asked me to stop shouting. How could I? I was drowning! I was angry! I was scared! I was not the same person I was before all of this started. Damn them all!

A barrage of new tests took place. One of the tests was endoscopy where some kind of dye was put inside Vas so they could follow its path and determine where the problem was. The doctor who was performing the procedure was one of the doctors that was looking after her at the time and took offence to my complaint. He was quite rough with her. When she came out she was in tears. She told me that she was in pain because no sedative was given to her and he was quite rough with her. I chose not to follow it up. Things were moving in the right direction, with the new tests.

That doctor treated me like a naughty child. He was rude and very rough with me. He did not sedate me and he rammed the camera down my throat, without any empathy or regard as to what I had just been through. The nurse looked shocked, bless her. When the test finished and he left, she tried to comfort me as best as she could. I was bawling my eyes out. I am quite a forgiving person; if I could go back today and see that man, I would floor him and do to him what he had done to me. He was a monster!

Anyway, back in my room, with my family around me, I felt a lot safer.

A psychologist came to assess me, to see if I was crazy. I told her, "I have got my son fighting for his life at Gillingham Hospital. I want to get better, so I can be with him! He needs me! I am not crazy. I am not suffering from depression. My problem is physical. You are all wrong."

Even with the new tests, Vas continued to deteriorate. We were in a downward spiral and we could not seem to be able to get out of it.

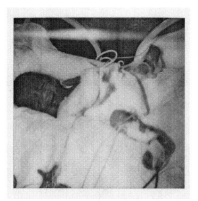

There they were; Vas with tubes in her in one hospital wasting away and Petros in another with more tubes and a bleak future, fighting for his life on a minute by minute basis. There I was in good health ending up being a mere spectator in the fight for survival of the two people that were my family and with a big question mark, as to how long they would continue to be.

They say when you are bad in life and you die, you go to Hell. Well, Hell did not want to wait for me. Hell had decided to come early. It came while I was still alive. I was in my own Hell every minute of every miserable day and there was not a damned thing I could do about it. The only thing I could do was watch as events carried on steadily unfolding around me; not much of a contribution for a so called protector of his family.

Petros had tubes inserted in him all over his body. They pierced him that much that some veins could not be used. He still could not breathe on his own and he had oxygen constantly pumped into him by the ventilator. Even with the ventilator continuously pumping air in him the alarms were going off. This scene was non-stop for weeks on end. Every now and then a consultant would approach me and tell me that I should not get my hopes up. If he survived this, he would most probably spend the rest of his life in a vegetative state. If he was functional, he would most probably have learning difficulties. He would most definitely not have a normal life.

We were living minute by minute; day by day and he was telling me about the future. My attitude was, let's get through today. When tomorrow comes, we shall deal with whatever it brings us. Petros was struggling to stay alive from one hour to the next, which was our immediate problem. Now was not the time to discuss possible future outcomes.

Vas was not getting better, either. I could only face today's problems. Tomorrow would come soon enough, with its own problems and special shitty surprises.

Luckily before Vas fell ill, with the help of a pump we stored some of her milk. The nurses were putting some in a syringe, with which they would pass it on to Petros through a tube. At least he was getting some of Vas's nutrients and anti-bodies through that. To give you an idea of how much milk they gave him, if I was to swallow it, it would not have covered a quarter of my tongue. He was that small. But in retrospect, a normal, healthy baby's stomach is only the size of a thimble at birth, so Petros' must have been no larger than a hollowed-out penny. My luck, penny!

From a happy go lucky person, I turned into a person I did not recognize. There was always a frown on my face. Apart from Vas, I was quite snappy and abrupt with everyone. I think there was an angry aura and a crazed, desperate look on my face that kept people at arm's length from me. Whenever someone dared to tell me that I should have faith and not to worry because they were sure both Vas and Petros were going to be alright, I wanted to beat them up so badly. Their stupid crystal balls and religion!

The way I can try and describe how I was feeling, is if you can imagine someone a lot stronger than you, is pushing your head in a bathtub full of water. You are helpless and just before you drown he lets you come up, gasping for air—I think it's called 'Water-boarding'. As soon as you take your first breath, your head is submerged in the water again. This happens continuously with the duration of how many breaths you take, the only changing factor. It happens for so long, that you are hoping that mercy will be shown to you or that you will be left to die, so that you are put out of your misery. This is what it felt we were going through since we started the IVF and eventual birth. Life threatening scares, frights and more bloody scares…all this in such a short period of time. At least when we were trying to fall pregnant there was nothing life threatening. I thought it was a miserable time back then. How I longed for that time again; all this craziness from a romantic dream of wanting to have a baby to be transformed into a hateful, angry and antisocial monster!

⌐/⌐

Arrangements were made for Andrea to be transported back to our local hospital, in the morgue. At the last minute, our local hospital cancelled the transportation, claiming that something on the forms was not okay, or words to that effect. I was asked by Gillingham Hospital, if I could transport her. The whole thing was ludicrous. Of course I said yes. I had to drive that whole two-hundred miles with my deceased daughter lying in a box next to me. I put the box with Andrea in it, on the passenger seat. Quite honestly, I just could not help myself; I opened the box and saw her lying there. I cried. Father and daughter were taking their first and last trip together.

When I reached the hospital, I had to drive round the back, where I had to knock on the door. That was where they kept the cadavers. I knocked on the door, someone opened it and I told them who I was. They took the papers that I was holding and the box that Andrea was lying in and unceremoniously closed the door in my face. It was so cold and inhuman.

I made my way back to Gillingham, wondering if I was going to be asked to make a second trip. I knew that a second trip with Petros would have meant the end of my wife. A possible scenario for my second trip would have been me, crashing on the motorway barrier just to end it all. That was the depth of my despair!

No new treatment or medicine was given to Vas after the tests. Even after all the tests they found nothing, which reinforced their original diagnosis of severe post-natal depression.

Various people (parents and relatives of other babies) at different times tried to talk to me. They were reaching out to bond with others in a similar situation to themselves. They picked the wrong person as my only response to them was an angry and deranged glare. I was on the brink of losing everything I held dear and they had the audacity to try and have small talk with me. You see, for me every day was not a day that I could say Vas and Petros were getting better or stronger. Every miserable day, was just another day where both of them deteriorated and I did not know for how long I was going to be a husband and a father. I just could not care less about them or their families. Very quickly everyone stopped trying to talk or even look at me, which suited me just fine. I was in a cesspit of hate, anger, misery and despair and the rest of the human race was irrelevant to me nor had any need for it. It was a dark, lonely and cold place to be marooned at. Welcome to my bloody world!

My mother in law wanted to ask the priest to come and give Vas a blessing and Holy Communion. We did not think that she was going to last much longer if this condition continued. She lost so much weight. Her organs inside seemed to have packed up. My mother in law felt that since all the medical tests failed, it would be good for Vas to have the Holy Communion. She only mentioned it once, but as I chose to ignore her, she did not ask me again. As far as she was concerned, I did not say no. To be honest, the reason I ignored her was because they were still clinging on to their stupid religion and beliefs and I was not in the right frame of mind to argue in a civilized manner. So I assumed, the fact that I ignored her, she would get the message and drop it. The other reason was that by allowing that, it felt to me that I was giving up on Vas as at that confused time I thought she was referring to Last Rites.

I was wrong wasn't I? Unknown to me, the priest was asked to visit and he readily accepted. By me not actually saying 'no', my mother-in-law felt that on that technicality, she was within her right to bring in the priest. I think she would have brought him anyway, as she was in pain, from seeing her daughter in that state. This is something I did not appreciate at the time or understood, as I was consumed by my own grief. I felt that I was alone and the whole fucking world was against me.

There I was in the room, sitting on the side of Vas's bed. The room was quiet as Vas was asleep and I was having a great time (not!) being lost in my own miserable thoughts. The room was dark as the curtains were drawn. I heard some loud voices outside, which I ignored. The door opened suddenly, without anyone knocking. I jumped out of my skin. All I saw was the silhouette of a tall creature wearing some kind of flowing clothes, looking quite menacing. Suddenly the light was switched on. I don't know if you have ever seen a Greek priest. They are dressed in black with a black cap on their head and a long beard. He scared the Hell out of me. He looked like the Grim Reaper. This tall man, all dressed in black just entered the room without knocking. That was one more of my mother-in-law's technicalities. By me not saying 'no' at the beginning, whether the priest could come or not, she felt that she could bring him in without giving me the chance to refuse. This way it was too late for me to say no.

After my heart settled down from the scare, my mother-in-law made the introductions. I was fuming. I glared at her but she chose to ignore me. I was not impressed to say the least.

I woke Vas up and after she sat up in bed, he performed the blessing which I did not understand as most of the words they use are ancient Greek. He then proceeded to give Vas the Holy Communion. She looked lethargic and uncomfortable as she was continuously in pain. Now, because of my mother-in-law's sly use of technicalities, I felt that it was unfair for Vas to be woken up and having to endure a religious process, which she would not have understood anyway. I was hoping that it would not have taken long.

Would I have let him in, if I knew? I think so, as religion is important to Vas. That was the one and only reason. Nevertheless, I intended to have a few words with my mother-in-law later. Her free use of technicalities, to get around me, was increasing. I had enough to worry about, without having to wait and see what surprise she would spring up next. One thing I was never tolerant of was people interfering in our lives, irrespective of who they were. I was very angry at that moment. When I am angry I refrain from putting words to my thoughts.

Words will come out of your mouth when you are angry and once spoken can never be taken back. My policy was to talk about what made me angry, after I calmed down. I felt it was more constructive and less hurtful. My mother-in-law would just have to wait. The way I was feeling, it would have taken years for me to calm down; it is a good job I am extremely patient.

✧

I had not eaten for weeks. I was a shadow of my former self. I had my baby fighting for his life in another hospital and I was unable to go and see him there. I was on a constant drip and was being fed intravenously. It was the most important time of my life and I had no control over my body, but then again who does? I was wasting away and only through my faith I kept my sanity. I could tell that my husband was worried for both Petros and I but it was out of anyone's hands. The doctors were baffled with my condition.

I felt that the top part of my body was separated from the bottom part; the top part being the bottom part of my chest. Whatever I ate or drank would be puked up soon after. It was as if there was a trap door and the food and liquids had nowhere to go. A junior doctor came in my room to sympathetically tell me that I was indeed suffering from severe post-natal depression and of course I did not know it. They just did not know what was wrong with me. It was physical and not mental. I tried to tell them this, but it fell on deaf ears. I was so weak and wasting away. I gave birth to my son and I still did not get to hold him in my arms and welcome him to this world. I was feeling sick and helpless.

When the priest came to bless me, he gave me Holy Communion. As soon as I swallowed it, I felt God's healing hands working their magic.

It was something out of this world! It was like hot hands, spreading across every single part of my body. I have not experienced anything like that since.

About an hour or so after the priest had gone; I actually felt whatever was in the wrong place (in my body), go back in its right place. It was as if a knot, was being untangled. I turned to Steve, and told him, "I am going to be okay now". I could tell that he was humoring me by agreeing with me. He has been scarred by the whole process and priests and the church were considered by him to be a joke. Nonetheless I was positive. I knew I was going to walk out of that room and go and see my son. I most definitely was! Steve was going to get there in his own time. That is the point of Free Will. At that time he had his stubborn streak in him for which I did not blame him.

<hr>

According to Vas, when she swallowed the Holy Communion she felt something warm go throughout her whole body. She felt that she was going to get better. I was skeptical because at the time God and priests were not on the top of my friends list. I smiled and agreed with her, still despairing and believing in nothing. My whole world was falling apart and there was nothing I could do. My wife held on to her religious beliefs when there was no logical reason to do so. She was in the thick of it, so there was no chance that she did not realize that life sucked and that religion was something that was invented for the masses as a controlling opiate. As far as I was concerned, if that helped her to get through this nightmare, good luck to her. I never discouraged her or made any negative remarks about her beliefs. She never tried to influence me to become religious, either. It is a personal choice and should always be one.

Was she wrong, about her religious beliefs? Of course she was. It was very easy for me to dismiss religion, considering what we had gone through and were still going through. If her God was kind and malevolent, I did not see a glimpse of that. If he really existed, he was not the kind that Vas thought he was. If he was the kind that I thought he was; I did not particularly want to get to know him.

The most important thing to understand here is that we started our first IVF one and a half years before. During that very short period we had three attempts on IVF. We lost two babies. The third was fighting for his life and I had my wife fighting for hers as well. During that period I made bad decisions and I was not a very good husband to Vas. I experienced rage, hate and helplessness of immense proportions.

That experience changed me into a monster.

We come to the surprising bit. Within two hours the puking seemed to have slowed down. Vas could still not eat or drink anything. But she was more alert and kept saying that she knew that she was going to be alright. There was a spark in her eyes. However the rest of her body was telling me otherwise.

Bless her, she was a shadow of her former self but still kept her faith. The puking lessened but there was no evidence as far I could see that she was going to recover. She started to actually smile and countless times tried to reassure me that she was absolutely confident that with God's help, she was going to be fine. She kept telling me that since she had the Holy Communion, she was confident she was going to walk out of there. That is why she is my beacon. That is why, while she is in my life there is a chance I am going to be a better person.

This situation continued for two days. She could still not eat, but she had a smile on her face. Was she in the same room as me? Was she seeing the same things as me? Of course she was. Did the priest put some kind of drug in the communion? Physically there was no improvement but mentally she was sharp and happy. She was actually happy! She kept telling me over and over again that with God's help she knew she was going to be by Petros' side. She had been away from him too long. Was she delusional or was I too stupid and stubborn to see what was happening in front of me?

Coming face-to-face with such resolute and unyielding faith made me take a step back and take stock of my situation. Vas went through all that pain, lost two babies; one fighting for his life and her close to dying and she was still holding to her belief that there is a God. I honestly believe that Vas is a better human being than me. For her to still believe, made me put aside my anger and hate and actually reconsidered my theory about the existence of God.

There were not a lot of private places around nor did I know or care if there was a chapel in the hospital. I found the first available bench and sat down. I was not worried that anyone was going to come and sit next to me or talk to me. I think by that time, word got round that I was an obnoxious and ignorant jerk as I ignored any attempt of conversation with anyone with just a single menacing glare. I closed my eyes…I pictured myself in church…I wanted to connect…I wanted to believe…I wanted even just a fraction of what my wife believed. In my mind I got on my knees and prayed.

That was, when for the first time in my life I got closer to God. That was when in private (public!) I got on my knees and prayed to God to save my wife and son. Some of the hate and aggression I had, seemed to have lifted. Not a lot, mind you. I had enough to fill an ocean. I fervently wanted to believe.

I could not hear or feel, anything around me. It was so peaceful. For those seconds or minutes…(I honestly cannot remember how long I was there) my troubles, scares and worries were washed away. I was in a plateau of tranquility, love and contentment. I wanted to stay there, for there was a feeling of belonging.

It was not dramatic, where I could have claimed to have seen a vision or heard a voice! All I got was a peaceful feeling and a sense of belonging. Knowing how I turned out to be that last year, it was not a small feat.

There has to be something more in this world than just us. There has to be some kind of plan. Whether you are a Christian, a Muslim, a Buddhist, etc. there has to be a higher force and some of the struggles we go through now will not last forever.

I made my private pact with God, took courage and prepared myself to face the daunting realities of that day, with a new resolve. I knew the future was bleak but I had to remain positive. This was not a one minute conversion from atheist/agnostic to believer. It takes time and a lot of humility. I wished I had time and as for humility, I had a lot of work to do there.

During that time not a single person sat next to me or tried to talk to me while I was sitting there!

I only had to go as far back as the day before. Any mention from anyone that they found God…would have immediately resulted in me thinking, "Delusional, jerk, idiot…" Some of you might be thinking the same thing about me now as well. The only thing I can say is, "God bless you all". This is the point of Free Will.

I am the wrong person to talk to you about faith. I have found what you would call peace inside me. I was quite an angry person at the time. Accepting that there is a greater force around us and that we are not here alone facing our daily trials gave me strength. Deep, very deep inside me there was a glimmer of hope that we were going to return home intact as a family. We might have to face a lot more struggles but there was a chance. It was a nice feeling. I wish you all get to experience it—or don't in the case of our account. Don't get me wrong, I am not telling you that I have become a devout Christian all of a sudden…far from it. I am flawed and as a result I still have my doubts. What I am trying to tell you is that I have accepted God in my heart and into my life and it is a nice feeling. I have got a long way to go before I can call myself religious, but I am on the right track. It's a process of baby steps.

The situation was still bleak but bearable.

I told Vas the private pact I made with God and she was angry with me. Apart from her I never told it to anyone else nor do I intend to do so now. When I made it I meant it and still do.

My word is my bond.

Do not forget that I was a long way from home. I lived on takeaway food. Eating by myself just extended my misery and loneliness. So, as Vas kept saying that she was feeling better, I brought my pizza in the room to eat it there. What an insensitive and stupid thing to do. I got an earful from her and with my tail between my legs I took the pizza and left the room. She was still on the drip and the smell made her nauseous. To actually start eating in front of a person, who had not eaten for weeks, speaks volumes about my sensitive and caring nature—or the latter in this case!

In the meantime nothing medically new was given to Vas. She was still on a drip and being fed intravenously. As far as the doctors were concerned, she was still suffering from severe post-natal depression, as their subsequent tests revealed nothing to contradict that theory.

One day, just like that, Vas let out a mighty fart. That was one stinky and loud fart. That was the mother of all farts. That was the first day of her recovery. To this day we don't know what was exactly wrong with her.

A few days went by and Vas started having soups and gradually going onto solid foods. She was getting better and stronger.

I was so relieved. Vas took it in her stride. For her, there was no question about her getting better. She was just anxious to be able to walk out of that room and go and be with Petros.

The doctor's explanation then, was that Vas could have had a severely twisted bowel which of course they missed. It goes without saying that they were still not sure what was wrong with her. They conveniently forgot their original assessment of severe post-natal depression and their lack of care to determine and solve the problem. I did not forget, but as my wife was getting better, I never brought it up.

One down, one to go; it was Petros' turn to pull through. I was sure that a fart would not have solved his problem. If only it was as simple as that.

I decided never to have that talk with my mother-in-law. Her heart was in the right place and she meant well. She actually helped Vas by bringing the priest. What are a few technicalities between family members as long as they are not made out of malice? She will be pleasantly shocked when she reads this!

We reached the point where Vas had the strength to visit Petros for the very first time. She had to see him with her own eyes. It had been so long for her.

She broke down in tears when she saw that Petros had still got tubes and needles in him. He looked so small and fragile. That was the first time she managed to hold him in her arms. Then the tears of joy followed. She was actually holding our son. It was a delight to see Vas holding Petros. This was a scene that with all the mayhem going around me I never thought I would get to see. The mother walking out of her room on her own two feet and the son staying alive long enough to be held by her.

Whether Petros survived or not, by us just reaching that point, was a miracle in itself. It makes you humble, thankful and hopeful. If we managed to reach that point, then there was a chance that we would hopefully manage to achieve our dream; one difficult step at a time. Petros had to survive long enough to get stronger.

It was such a great boost to our morale. It made a change from the usual frights and scares. Just for that precious moment the frown that seemed to have embedded itself on my face vanished.

Life is so fragile. We always plan for tomorrow. We never stop to think that just like that, there could be no tomorrow due to a heart attack or accident…Embrace today and enjoy the little things that you are faced with. Tomorrow, if it comes, will come soon enough.

This is how my outlook on life changed that day. Gone were the plans to open and own multiple fish and chip shop outlets. I was working long hours as it was. My plans now were to be there for my family from that day forwards; God willing, the day after and the day after that. However this journey of ours ended: Vas and Petros, or just Vas, would need me to be there. Actually be there and not just in words. As Vas used to tell me, "Life is what you make of it…" Whenever she wanted to go somewhere and I could not because of work, I did not feel guilty as work came first. She was not impressed with my attitude but she never complained.

Seeing her walk out of that miserable room and hold our son, against all odds, changed me; Live for today. Be happy. Be kind, loving and giving to your loved ones. Once they are gone your plans and money are useless. All you will be left with is a series of different variations of, "If only I had the chance to tell them…show them… be there for them…" We have only one shot at this life. What kind of legacy do you want to leave behind? My revised legacy is; family comes first, second and third. Everything else is not that important in the grand scheme of things.

When you are feeling hard done by, take a quick visit to your nearest hospital; you will immediately realize, that your life is not as bad as you thought. There are lots of people worse off than you. Enjoy your family and what you have around you, for you do not know, how long you or they will be around.

The day mummy got out of
Margate Hospital
OUR FIRST CUDDLE !!

As you can see from the picture above, that was the first time I got to hold my son. It felt such a long time ago since I had given birth. My heart ached. He was so tiny. He was so light. He still had needles in his hands and legs. The monitors kept bleeping every time he stopped breathing. That moment was special. Even though in my case it came late, it was priceless nonetheless. All the troubles we had gone through were worth it to just reach this point. I just prayed for my little soldier to have the strength to fight and stay alive. Even though every day he stayed alive was a blessing, he actually got a little bit stronger and bigger, thus increasing his chances of survival.

He just had to. Any other outcome would have destroyed me mentally. I tried not to dwell on the worst possible scenarios and just kept looking at the little victories. That's what kept me going. Every hour and every day he stayed alive was extra strength that was built in his body, to fight for the next hour and next day. That was enough for me. Bless him. He was so little. He looked so fragile.

―✑―

One evening while we were visiting Petros, he seemed to have problems breathing…more so than normal. The alarms kept going off and the poor, tireless nurses kept running to him. It was very distressing to see him like this. But that was not enough, was it? The fire alarm went off. A utility room in the hospital caught fire and we had to evacuate, leaving Petros behind as he could not survive outside the high dependency unit. When we went outside we could see black smoke coming from the top of the roof. The fire brigade was on the scene in minutes. This roller coaster had gone beyond funny now. How much more could we humanly take? Thankfully, it was put out quite quickly. When we went upstairs later, we were happy to see that neither the fire nor the fumes had reached Petros' unit. Small blessings. They put out the fire before it got out of control. To say that we were shaken, it is an understatement.

You had to be in our shoes to understand us. I know the fire was put out quickly. Those ten minutes though were long. To my shame, it never even crossed my mind to worry about the other babies in that unit or the other ill patients who could not be moved. All I was thinking was Petros.

We would take a sigh of relief when a scare we went through was over, but then there was always something life-threatening that would pop up and take years off our lives. It was not one or two. It was constant. It was as if someone was using a chisel on us, chipping away a piece at a time. By default you become a wreck and weak. You reach a stage that even the tiniest problem becomes overwhelming.

―✑―

Babies that were admitted to the Neo Natal unit after Petros were going home. We were still there. Each day that Petros survived, we were thankful to God. He just had to hang in there, fill up and get stronger. He just had to! He was getting the best possible care. I was hopeful. Vas was on the mend and getting stronger. There was some sort of peace inside me. Don't get me wrong. I was still worried to near-death. However they were increasing the duration my little soldier was breathing on his own! He had setbacks but the medical staff persevered…so did he! They kept increasing the times. He just had to tough it out until he could hold his own and breathe by himself. It was a relentless and constant battle that he had to overcome. It was simply a matter of life and death.

The alarms would go off and the nurses would rush over to him. When he was settled they would take him off the ventilator again. It was a battle that he had to win if he was to have any chance of survival. His chances kept increasing each day he survived, for he was getting stronger. His little body was filling up. It was amazing. It was a miracle! His eyes were open. I could see his nipples! Yes, they eventually formed. He was looking like you would expect a baby to look, but on quite a smaller size. He was the light at the end of the tunnel and it was steadily getting stronger.

I actually started to have conversations with the other parents on the ward. Some of them were a bit apprehensive at the beginning as they still thought I was an ignorant jerk. It was just small talk about the progress of our babies…That was the first step in me joining the human race, from 'jerk land'. I still held them at arm's length though. Baby steps!

For the first time in those miserable eighteen months, I felt that there was hope for us. Vas was getting better and Petros was getting stronger as they were increasing the duration that he was breathing on his own. My family; my unit was on the mend. For the first time ever, I actually felt that I was going to be a father and that there would be no more trips to the cemetery.

Did I forget about the doctor that delayed Vas's Caesarean? Of course not. Did his negligence cause the death of Andrea? Yes! Most probably! Maybe! I do not know! I could have played an endless list of possible scenarios reflecting his negligence, but I still could not be sure. His negligence could be said that it gave Petros the necessary few hours to come out alive. I am in a better place now, that I can forgive. Had Petros not survived our family would have crumbled. I would not have found God. There would have been no Vas to reign me in. I would have made it my life's mission to bring Hell to that doctor while he was still alive. I would have made sure, his life ended up being more miserable than mine. I was in a very bad place during that period and I would have sure as Hell, made sure I dragged him in that Hell with me.

As it stands I am lucky and so is he. Let's leave it at that. I do hope he learned from this mistake and did not inflict any pain on any other family.

Chapter 11

Promotion

The day came when Petros got a promotion. He was transferred to the adjacent unit, which indicated he did not need a twenty-four-hour care. We were cautiously optimistic. He was left to breathe on his own. He had setbacks sometimes, but there was definitely progress in the right direction. Our little miracle was getting stronger. He was still small and fragile, but to me he looked like a little lion trying to rise and be heard. He fought and never gave up. His very presence kept both my wife and I sane and hopeful. He was our light at the end of the tunnel and day by day that very light was getting stronger. God bless him.

There was a stark difference to the whole atmosphere between the Neo Natal and his new unit. First of all there were not so many nurses.

Their main job was to monitor more than anything else. There were not so many monitors either. The atmosphere was more relaxed. Petros was left breathing on his own. For the first time, it was he who was in control of his own lungs. It was a joy to go and see him. He was on the right track to recovery.

We were informed that they were ready to release Andrea's body for burial. Vas and I drove back home, while my in-laws stayed with Petros. We stood there in tears, burying our second baby, which we did not get a chance to get to know. There was a flicker of light though. It was coming from two-hundred miles away, from Petros.

⌒⧸⌒

We buried Andrea in the same section of the cemetery as Xristos. It is a section just for babies. It is so sad to see the countless rows of babies who died during pregnancy or soon after they were born. It breaks my heart whenever I go there. It is a colorful place, full of little toys and flowers. It is a painful place, where you are reminded of your little angels you never got a chance to know and nurture. It is so sad!

⌒⧸⌒

We managed to drive back in one piece. Vas was in tears all the way. It was such a boost to see Petros again. We could see his little chest going gently up and down. Gone were the violent chest movements because of the HFOV ventilator.

The HFOV ventilator! We needed God's help as well as science.

King's College London 19/03/2014 News:

Babies born extremely prematurely are at a high risk of developing breathing problems as their lungs are not yet mature and can be damaged by the breathing support that is needed to keep them alive.

Breathing support can be provided by conventional ventilation, which assists their breathing at their breathing rate, or by high-frequency oscillatory ventilation (HFOV). During HFOV smaller, shorter bursts of gas are delivered which may be less damaging to their fragile lungs and therefore may reduce the chronic respiratory problems experienced by babies born very prematurely…

Irrespective of the potential dangers for Petros being on the HFOV ventilator, that was the best thing for him. That rapid and constant force of oxygen in the lungs was what kept him alive to live and fight another day. I don't think he would have survived otherwise. We were so lucky that he was picked second out of Vas's belly. He was so lucky. That decision I made out of ignorance and desperation proved to be the correct one. A small but significant victory! We started having a few victories, but we were far from winning the war.

Vas would change his diaper and give him drops of milk or water. Vas had still not fully recovered but motherhood suited her. She took to it, like a duck to water.

The amount of liquids he was getting was still very small. Vas would pick him up and hold him. I took me a while to do that. All kinds of crazy thoughts were stopping me. What if I dropped him? What if I held him too tight and suffocated him? All kinds of irrational thoughts were flying around my head. I was content, looking at Vas holding him. After a few days Vas was insistent. I had to let go of my stupid fears and hold him.

When I picked Petros up for the very first time, it was unreal. He was so small. He was so light that I had to look at him to make sure that I was still holding him. His skin was still a little bit dark. I looked at his hands and my heart melted. This brave little boy had marks all over from the needles. I quickly handed him to Vas. Baby steps! I felt I needed to do it slowly. I did not want to harm him by any clumsy action on my part. We had come this far. I felt that I could wait.

After a couple of more weeks in that ward, they wanted to release Petros from the hospital and transfer him to the Queen's Hospital. It is our local hospital in Burton-upon-Trent. They felt that he was stable enough because he was breathing on his own. That did not mean we were out of the woods yet. We were against it, but they were adamant as it was costing our local NHS Trust money having Petros cared by another hospital, when they could do the job themselves. We offered to pay and keep him there. They declined.

A transfer date was set and the ambulance came to pick him up, for the 200 mile journey back home. Petros was put in an incubator and fastened tight in the ambulance with a nurse and Vas joining him at the back. I was following in my car. I had a bad feeling about this. Anything could happen on a motorway. We have come this far and because of money they were putting Petros at risk. When we reached the M2 motorway, they pulled in for a stop at a service station. They spent a few minutes looking at the petrol station and then they pulled out and rejoined the motorway. At the next service station they pulled in again. The same thing again! I stopped my car alongside the ambulance and asked them what was wrong. Apparently they were low on petrol but the card they had to fill up, was not accepted by this petrol station either. An ambulance without enough petrol to reach its destination! Our ambulance service at its finest. I took £70.00 pounds out of my pocket and asked them to fill it up. Can you believe the sheer stupidity of the situation?

Later on, on the motorway they had to stop sharply which sent the nurse flying over at the back, bruising her legs and arms.

Eventually we reached the hospital.

Normally I would have been ready to pick up a fight for this kind of negligence. The ambulance should have been filled with petrol before they came to pick my son up. It did not require high levels of IQ. They were lucky I was a different person now after the months of the angry-Steve before. I was angry, but I was forgiving as well now. I did not file an official complaint neither did I make any angry phone calls. Vas was impressed. I was shocked by my own actions as well. The important thing was that we arrived safe and sound, albeit with a few bruises. In the grand scheme of things, that was a victory.

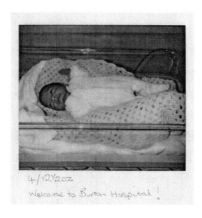

4/12/202
Welcome to Burton Hospital!

At the new hospital, they ran things different to how we were used to in Medway Maritime Hospital. Every day I would go there with a list of questions. I knew I was becoming irritating to them but I could not help it. Eventually we became friends with the head of the Baby Unit. Whenever he saw me in the corridor, he would pretend he was trying to hide to avoid my list of questions for the day. That doctor was quite helpful in putting my mind at ease regarding the care Petros was receiving at Queens Hospital.

Petros was getting stronger by the day.

The time was getting near when they thought Petros could be taken home. That was a day I never thought I would get to see. They were actually considering of discharging him!

They detected that Petros had a hernia. They wanted to discharge him and for us to bring him in at a later date as an outpatient. We refused. We would not take him home unless he had the operation. The operation was done at the Children's Hospital in Birmingham.

Before we left Queen's Hospital, Petros was given a hearing test. It came back as refer. We needed to make an appointment at the hospital in Nottingham where they specialize for these kinds of tests. I insisted on being given an apnea mat for Petros' bed, at home. They told me that there was no need, but I was adamant. The function of the apnea mat is when a baby is lying on it and he/she does not breathe for a specific time the alarm goes off to warn you; most of the times it is just that the baby takes a bit longer than usual to breathe. However, I wanted it with us, as Petros' early life was full of breathing problems. It is better to err on the side of caution. The hospital relented and gave us an apnea mat to take with us. Unknown to me at the time that was the best thing I had decided to be stubborn about.

Chapter 12

Going Home

The very first day we took Petros home was extremely exciting and vividly scary. I was excited that I was finally able to bring my son home, but at the same time, I was scared because I had to look after him by myself. I was a first-time mother. His whole wellbeing rested on me. Up to that moment there were doctors and nurses around; it was just the three of us now and with Steve working long hours, he could not help a lot. It was a daunting and scary task in those first weeks. I think if I had not gone through all the scares of the past few months I would have been more confident.

It was amazing as to how at the very beginning I expected my pregnancy to be and also how my giving birth was. Reality is always different and harsher than fantasy. I pictured myself falling pregnant after making love *with my husband. Reality in my case was IVF. I pictured myself pushing my baby out the normal way. Reality, in my case, was an emergency Caesarian. I pictured myself lying in a hospital bed, just as soon as I had given birth, holding my baby in arms; reality in my case was for my baby to be transferred to the Neo Natal High Dependency Unit, fighting for survival. I pictured myself spending a couple of days in hospital and then taking my son home; reality in my case was to be separated from my baby and being ill myself.*

These things can knock your confidence. I just had to take it one step at a time, and God willing, I would turn out to be a good mother.

Petros was released from hospital the date that he was supposed to be born, had Vas gone full term. He had spent his first three and a half months in the above two hospitals. It does not sound a lot. Those months were very long for us as they were full of scares.

He was still a tiny thing. While lying in his cot his apnea monitor would go off because he was not breathing regularly.

He was breathing on his own but to his own speed.

I remember the following day my mom called me at the shop asking me if Vas and Petros were alright. I told her they were alright and that she should call the house.

She told me she did, but there was no answer.

I called Vas later and a little sharply asked her why she was not answering the phone earlier when my mom was calling. She explained to me, in a sharp way as well, that Petros was difficult to feed and would not go to sleep easy. She had her hands full in dealing with Petros and she could not answer the phone whenever it rang.

Now, I should have realized that without making it an issue. Vas was a first-time mother with no family nearby to help. I was working long hours, so I was not much help either. Feeling stupid, I told Vas to go about what she had to do and not to worry about answering the phone.

Anyone who wanted to get updates had to call me. Vas had a twenty-four hour job with Petros and I failed to see it. I thought that I was the one who was working harder of the two of us. Looking after a baby is the hardest job you can do. I was still adapting. You would think I would have got it right by now.

A couple of nights later as I was working at the shop, the phone rang. A customer wanted to place his order. As I was talking to him, I heard the bleep in the line, indicating there was a call waiting. I was on the extension phone, so I did not know who was calling. I don't know how or why, but I felt an overwhelming urge to answer that call. Uncharacteristic on my part, I cut the conversation short. To this day I have never done that before. When the next call came through, all I heard was "Steve, Steve our baby. Our baby…"

That was my wife on the phone. There was so much despair and anguish in her screams. So much pain and helplessness! Panicky and fearing the worst I asked her what was wrong. All I got was, "Steve, Steve, our baby, our baby…"

You get to hear a scream like this and I tell you, it destroys your soul. A husband should never hear a scream like that coming out of his wife. Your blood freezes. That is one scream I never want to hear for the rest of my life.

Time was of the essence. Vas was in no condition to communicate with me. Whatever was happening must have been really bad. I went all cold and thought of the worse. I asked Vas to put the phone down and call an ambulance. I didn't know whether she heard me or not. I gave the keys to a member of staff and without any explanation I rushed out.

There was no need to explain to them. By now they knew, that by me doing that thing, it must have been an emergency. I got in my car and whilst driving I called the ambulance as well.

I was alone in the house with Petros. The apnea mat went off and I picked him up. I check him and he seemed alright. While I was holding him, I prepared his feed. I tried to get him to eat but he would not eat. While he was resting on me, I felt his heart rate and it seemed okay. His breathing seemed okay too. So I let Petros rest on me for a while until I tried to feed him again. As I was sitting on the rocking chair I heard a voice inside my head, "Check your son. NOW." Without thinking twice about it I lifted Petros from my shoulders and tried to check him out again. There, to my horror of horrors, I saw my son's face go grey and his eyes bulging out. I tried to talk to him and stimulate him but he went limp. He was not responsive. He was floppy in my arms. I panicked. I was hysterical. I called Steve straight away. To be honest I don't remember our conversation. I then called the emergency number where they dispatched an ambulance. I stayed on the phone with them. I was instructed to lay Petros on the floor and check his breathing. I quickly opened the front door, so the paramedics would just walk in and put my face next to Petros' nose to check if he was breathing. All the while, I was calling his name and shaking him gently. I felt as if I was losing my mind. I felt that what I was facing on the floor, was my third dead child. "Dear, God, whatever it is, help my son!"

I think there is a very thin line between sanity and madness. Madness was hovering above me, ready to grab me. If I was to have lost Petros, I would have gone mad, for dealing with reality would have been unbearable after that event.

He was looking lifeless. I really thought that my baby was dead. So much anguish and despair. The ambulance and Steve seemed to be taking forever.

Steve and the medics came in at the same time. I quickly told them what happened. After examining his vitals they gave him oxygen, carried him to the ambulance and raced straight back to the hospital, with us behind following in our car.

My blood froze. God, he looked awful. Was he dead? When was this torment going to stop? This is not a sight that any parent should see. This situation can break any parent. You bring your baby home for the first time and within the first few days you see him in that state, it breaks your spirit and confidence. We had already lost two. This was just too much.

Of course Vas was hysterical. How do you get over seeing your son lifeless? Again, don't forget, that we were first-time parents, with no relatives living near us for support. As we were following the ambulance at high speed, all kind of terrible thoughts were going through my mind. None of them had a good ending for Petros. While I was going through my terrible thoughts, I was trying to simultaneously make Vas snap out of her hysterical state. I was telling her that Petros was going to be alright. That did not work as I did not believe in the words I was saying myself.

I was close to snapping. Enough was enough. How much shit did we have to put up with? Why was it always us? Would Petros be dead by the time we reach the hospital? I was praying like never before. "Please God, let him live. Let him live and take me instead. Take me instead. What was the point of him surviving when he was so premature, for him to die now?"

The fact that I did not crash the car whilst following the ambulance was a miracle in itself. It felt as if I was speeding to face our doom, with a hundred meter cliff just round the corner. I felt crashed and defeated.

When we reached the hospital, they tried to delay us from seeing Petros. It must have been the way I looked at the nurse. I must have looked like a crazy person, ready to attack. She reconsidered and immediately let us in the room that they were treating Petros. I run over to him with Vas following. I was holding her hand and she had no option but to run as well. I was dreading it. I was expecting the worst.

There lying in the incubator was a small baby looking normal, with two doctors, who smiled when they saw us. I was not in a smiling mood. I kept looking at the baby, thinking they sent us in the wrong room. It took me a while to realize it was Petros. Vas was crying as soon as she saw him. Then it clicked. You see, I was expecting to see him as he was, when he was taken away from the house. Such a quick transformation. Petros was lying in the incubator as right as rain. All smiles and moving his arms, as if it was just a normal day.

The reason for this episode was this; Petros was given his immunization injections the day before. It was a delayed reaction to the injections, which scared us to death. His little body found them too much. They kept him overnight for observation. When we picked him up in the morning, he was his usually happy self, with happily no trace of what happened the night before. I prayed that night as I never had before. I was thankful! I was scared! I was relieved! Vas was shaken to her core! Who can blame her?

Emotionally, we were such as mess! You could have knocked us down with a feather. We found it so overwhelming and hard going! For us to be able to bring our son home after all our difficulties and after only two days with us, to be rushed to hospital, with us thinking he was going to die shook us to the core. Vas, bless her, is still haunted by this incident.

If I had a history of heart problems, I am sure I would have died of a heart attack. There is only so much anyone can take.

They say adversity brings you together. I felt we were close enough as it was. I was sure we did not need to get any closer. I just wanted a break. I wanted to lead a normal, boring life for a change.

Mr. Artley came to see us. He reassured us, that there was nothing to worry about. In life, it is not the grand gestures that count; it is the little acts of kindness. He did not have to come and see us. Once Vas fell pregnant, he successfully finished his job, with nothing else required from him. Nevertheless he came, as he did come at the beginning when Vas's ovaries ballooned to the size of balls. These little things show you the character and caring nature of a person. He may not have been lucky having us as his patients, but we were lucky to have him as our IVF consultant.

To this day whenever the phone rings I tense up. The instructions at the shop are, whoever is nearer to the phone, whether they are serving a customer or not, they have to stop and answer the phone immediately.

It had been about eighteen months, since we started our first IVF. Those months were long and hard. We had never experienced despair like that before in such heavy intensity. We were not the same naïve people. When we were in the thick of it, a picture of us being at home with a baby was one that never crossed my mind. That was truly a miracle. I would like to think that that experience made us humble and considerate towards everyone. There was and still is a lot of room for improvement for myself though!

We were lucky that we did not lose Petros that night. If he had died, it would have been explained as one more cot death. I am glad I insisted on having the apnea mat. There was no way I was going to give it up without a fight.

We got into a routine. Petros was difficult with drinking his milk. I would come home from work about eleven o'clock at night and I would do the one o'clock in the morning feed. I would give him his milk and when I tried to get him to burp, he wouldn't burp. As there was only a little bit of milk left in the bottle, I would take the chance to let him finish it and try to burp him again at the end. He would then throw up all the milk on me and on the settee. The first few nights I woke Vas up to change his diaper. After getting her up every night, Vas told me that she might as well do the feed herself, being that I kept waking her up. You see, it took her a couple of hours to fall asleep after I woke her up. I would finish with Petros' feed, get into bed and fall asleep straight away, while she was still awake.

She was with him all day, and silly me, I found it difficult to change a dirty diaper. I ate humble pie and the following night I gave him his milk and changed his diaper, enabling Vas to get some sleep. It was horrible but I still did it. Even then I had to adapt from my old fashioned mindset. You have to keep adapting to the changing situations in your life. I knew I was going to work, working long hours every day, but bringing up a baby is exhausting.

You have to understand that I grew up within an environment where the man is the boss. When it was time to eat my dad would just sit at the table with everything brought to him. When he finished eating, he would just get up, without taking any plates to the sink. I thought it was cool. He still does not know how to operate the cooker and he never washed a plate in his life. I don't think he ever made himself a cup of tea or he even knows how it is done. Everything was done for him. It is not surprising that I always wanted to be like him, when I grew up. It is a good life. That's why I had to keep adapting. My father got away with it. I just needed to be steered in the modern ways.

The work a woman has to put in is unbelievable. Our work pales into insignificance to what mothers do. I never missed one of my night shifts with Petros and never woke Vas up to change his diaper again. I really do learn from my mistakes.

$$\sim\!\!\!/\!\!\sim$$

After a couple of months, the hospital asked for the apnea mat back, which we of course refused to return. Petros' breathing was still irregular and the apnea mat would go off at various times of the day and night.

Just imagine this; it's the middle of the night and the apnea mat goes off. We both then jumped out of bed and ran like crazy people expecting the worse. To our delight Petros was okay. We went back to bed and an hour later the same thing. Night after night, after night... Our underlying problem was that we were too scarred and scared. We always expected the worse.

The hospital then suggested that we get a portable monitor that was available from the Cot Death Society. They loan out monitors to parents whose babies have breathing problems, like Petros, free of charge. The only thing they ask is for people to give a donation after they finish with it. This way it helps the society to meet its running costs and hopefully buy more monitors. We kindly asked for one and only after we tested it, did we return the apnea mat to the hospital. The monitor was attached to Petros twenty-four-seven. Whenever we were out people did not have to look for us. They only had to follow the sound of Petros' monitor going off. He was breathing at his own pace, which the monitor totally disagreed!

We went through the first few months enjoying Petros. It was such a delight. Vas was in her element. She was the mother hen. It was such a pleasure to cuddle him and actually hold my own son. It was sad that we never got to do that with Xristos and Andrea. We never really got a chance to mourn their loss. The time would come for that as well. They are our little angels! God bless them both!

Unfortunately time waits for no one. Now was the time, when we had to face the warnings of the doctors should Petros have survived. When we tried to get him to sit, he would flop and lie on his side. He just could not sit. His upper body was wobbly. At that age babies were crawling and standing up, but our little soldier could not remain seated.

We agreed with Vas that given our track record, we were not going to try for another baby. Vas's prayers had been answered when she became a mother. I almost lost both of them. Next time, we might not be so lucky. We had our hands full, worrying about Petros' progress anyway. We decided that we should just focus on him. It might sound selfish, but we were both scarred and going through the process again was quite daunting. We did not know what problems we were going to face with Petros. As his parents, who brought him into this world, we owed him our unwavering and unquestioning attention. Until the day we die, we shall be responsible for him. It is as simple as that. We had to focus on him, no matter what. We are a unit.

Guess what? The people we met at functions were still voicing their insightful comments. We were worried to death, about Petros' inability to sit. Since he had this problem, together with the referral for hearing loss, we were dreading what other developmental problems he had to deal with. So, the main topic of all our conversations was always relating to Petros. He is our purpose in life after all.

At one of the functions we attended, a couple came over and started fussing over Petros. Before they came over to us, Vas and I were discussing whether we should take him to a specialist or just wait a bit longer.

Their first direct comment to us was, "It is about time, you give him a brother or a sister". As I said before, I have found some sort of peace inside me. For a few seconds I lost that peace. I really wanted to punch them so bad! They knew what we went through, but they still felt that they had to impart their wisdom on us. I whispered to Vas that I was going to the bar and left without talking to them. I only went back when they left.

The months that followed found Vas in her relentless manner forever trying to sit him up and make him smile. He was smiling alright but he was still unable to remain seated. It was a continuous battle with Vas. Failure was not an option.

There was just no upper body strength. Vas was the optimistic one. It was a long process but eventually months later; when Vas tried to get him to sit up he wobbled but did not fall on the side. He stayed sitting up. Vas called me at work. When I picked up the phone the first thing I heard was a scream from Vas saying "Yes, he's done it." All I heard was the scream. My blood froze. With a scared heart I quickly asked her what was wrong. Laughingly she told me that Petros could sit up now. Her excitement was obvious, but my heart was doing summersaults. Very calmly I told to her, never to call me again screaming with excitement, as in my panic I did not hear what she was telling me and my blood froze with fear, that something was wrong with her or Petros. I was still scarred from her call when Petros went grey and his eyes were bulging out. She understood and never repeated that again. It's all a process of understanding each other and adapting.

When I was calling Petros he would not respond. I remember that he had a referral about his hearing. When we took him to Nottingham, he was diagnosed as having severe loss of hearing. He just would not respond to the sounds they exposed him to. I was devastated. They gave us a hearing aid and suggested that we talk to him often, even though he might not be able to hear us. Well, I was determined. I would talk to him constantly. I would talk to him in a clear and concise manner.

It was a case of continuing how you started. Nothing was going to be easy. We had our next mountain to climb. One problem is sorted and another pops up. The only thing was that they were all big ones. The quality of his life would be determined by how he conquered or adapted to his various developmental challenges. They gave us a hearing aid which he did not like. He kept pulling it off. They then suggested that we put sticky tape on it and one end of the tape to be stuck on his hair, which would be painful for him to pull off. Obviously they did not know Petros that well. That did not deter him. He kept pulling it off resulting in a hairless patch behind his ear. He was stubborn. Vas was a lioness. He would pull the hearing aid off and Vas would put it back in his ear straight away. This thing went on continuously for ten days. Petros' hair behind his ear disappeared. He was stubborn but so was Vas. One of them had to give in. Petros finally gave in. Stubborn little bugger. He just did not want to go down without a fight.

Vas would talk to him constantly. Petros was not impressed. I think he still held a grudge about his hearing aid. He would not utter a single word. He just kept smiling. Vas persevered. Even though she was getting no response, this glorious woman, my beacon, never gave up. She kept it up for months on end. I think Petros must have gotten a headache by the constant barrage of words coming out of Vas, for one day just like that, he decided to say, "Dada". "That's my boy." The first ever word he said, was to call me. Vas called me straightaway. Calmly she told me that Petros spoke his first word, then, followed a barrage of screams of excitement from Vas, as Petros showed promise about overcoming the speech hurdle. We were not out of the woods yet, but it was a start. It was momentous. He could speak. If he could speak, then however miniscule, he could hear. Bless him. I wished his first word was, "Mommy". To first call his mom, who gave birth to him and almost died. I think he was repaying her for the hairless patch behind his ear. Every single day Vas was talking to him face to face. She was relentless. She was his mother, after all. Petros was always smiling. Deep down, I think he was thinking, "For God's sake, give me a break. You know I can talk. Take it easy." However he did not have a vote in the matter.

The first word that Petros said clearly was, "Dada". "My God. He can talk. He can hear." We were over the moon. He was obviously quite slow with his development, but better slow than never. "My angel spoke." I smothered him with kisses. I had such a big grin on my face. I continued our daily routine of talking to him, face to face. Of course one of the words that I kept repeating was mommy. You never know, he might decide to surprise me. It was a long and continuous process.

One morning as we were doing our daily routine of words, I thought I heard him say "Mama". I smiled as I thought it was wishful thinking on my part. He kept saying "Dada" every now and then and a few other half-words. I was patient.

Then it happened!

My son called me "Mamma". He uttered the word that I thought I would never get to hear. My heart melted. Words cannot describe the happiness that I felt. For the very first time after all those years I got to hear the word that I longed for. I smothered him with kisses. I was crying uncontrollably. I was happy. When I settled down, I calmly called Steve and told him. I did not want to scare him. After I told him what happened, I started sobbing and the tears ran like rivers. How I enjoyed those happy tears of utter contentment!

I felt at peace with myself. My own flesh and blood called me, "Mama". Knowing what we had been through, coming to this stage was a miracle in itself. Having heard my severely deaf baby call me, "Mamma", gave me strength that we could face any challenges with a reasonable expectation of success. However little, he could hear and after a lot of perseverance, he proved to us he that he could talk. It might be a long road, but we would soldier on. Having faith in God and supporting each other through thick and thin, I was confident that we could live a reasonably healthy and happy life. For everyone has their sad story. The happy face that you see on the street might not be the same face that you see in the house. We all suffer in one way or the other. Seek help and support and hopefully that will see you through.

Petros next venture was to crawl. He was fourteen months old by now. He found it quite exciting. After a few weeks of slowly learning the basics and crashing into a few chairs, he would move like a rocket. He was late again but there was not a lot we could do apart from encouraging him. Our problem was that we were always comparing his progress to other babies of a similar age. That was wrong, but we could not help it. The main thing was that he adapted. He was always late but as long as he got there, a bit of worry from us was a small price to pay.

When Vas tried to teach him how to walk, as soon as she let go he would immediately land on his bum. He just did not want to walk. We were concerned again because walking was another one of the problems that they said he might have difficulty with. You see now, every time he was late with his development we were petrified that indeed, it was a problem. When we were told not to worry…it was easier said than done.

Other babies could walk by the age of eight months, but ours was seventeen months old by now and still nothing. We really thought that we were going to have problems there. He was just too late with this one. It was just a matter of time when one the doctors' warnings materialized. We were lucky so far, but his inability to walk kept us on tenterhooks.

If Petros thought we were going to give in, he was wrong; Vas kept at him. Encouraging and bribing him to take the first step, so he can be rewarded with sweets and toys and us taking a sigh of relief. I suppose, if Petros was incapable of walking, we would have accepted it and adapted to it.

Thank God it did not come to that.

We were jubilant when at the age of eighteen months he took his first steps. Vas was continuously thanking God. She said that it was better than willing the lottery. At last, we ticked the line where it said walking.

The next day, Petros fell ill and never took another step for the duration of the illness.

A few days later, when he got better, Vas started to encourage him to walk again. He was having none of that. He would immediately land on his bum and start crawling. We knew he could walk, as Vas had seen him do it. She bribed him with sweets and toys again…Nothing, no result! Three months went by and still he never took a single step. We were concerned and baffled. Nothing could motivate him to walk. It was as if it never happened. Vas put all his toys on the chairs and the settee. He always had to grab on to something and stand in order to get a toy. However, he would not try to walk. Vas was patient and relentless. Every day, she would try to get him to take the first step. Petros was stubborn. Apparently he was not ready. He preferred to be picked up and carried.

We reached a stage where we were questioning ourselves as to whether Vas had really seen him walk and it was not a figment of her imagination. There was no improvement from that day, when she saw him walking three months before. He was twenty one months old now! Other babies were running by now. Not Petros. We must have imagined it! We were deflated and dispirited.

Apparently we did not get the memo from Petros. He was going to walk when he was good and ready and not when it was expected of him to do so. One day, just like that, when he was twenty two months old, he decided that he wanted to give walking another go. What a victory! He was a bit behind with his development, but better late than never. He was operating on his own time-table. Of course it took him a while to master the task. He looked like a drunken sailor the first few weeks. We encouraged him, but never pressured him. To this day we follow the same pattern.

He had a problem with his eyes and he had to start wearing glasses. His lenses are the wrong shape. By wearing the glasses, the problem was corrected. Considering the other problems that he had, this was not a big one; another one of the scares, but not so daunting.

I know that every step was a worry, but we were smiling now. Petros was growing up without any major problems. Whether he was slow in any particular development or not, it did not really matter. The world was a loving and happy place and we were content. We were watching our little miracle grow and be healthy. What else can a parent want?

For the very first time we were thoroughly enjoying him as a baby and nurturing him. It was heaven!

His early years were occupied with trips to Nottingham Hospital where he was being monitored for his hearing, also the Children's Hospital in Birmingham and the Queen's Hospital in Burton-upon-Trent.

When Petros went to preschool he was the oldest in his class. However he was the smallest. That worried me a lot. He had to get used to the noises in a big environment as he was only used to our very quiet environment. It was difficult at first but he adapted. He had to always sit at the front of the class so that his teacher's talking would not be lost on him from all the noises and talking of the other kids.

—/—

Petros missed a year from school by a few days. We were not worried about that, as that meant I would have him at home for an extra year. His first day at preschool, I dressed him and took him there. When I tried to leave, he was crying. I don't know who was crying more between the two of us. I stayed a bit longer and he was forever checking to see that I was still there. After a while, when I saw that he was engrossed in a game, I very quietly left with tears streaming down my cheeks. This went on for a few days. He got used to it. I did not. I still cried every time I left him behind at school.

—/—

I speak Greek and so does Vas. A lot of people told us to teach him Greek from an early age as kids pick up a language easier when they are young. We both agreed that it was an unnecessary stress on him as another one of the possible problems he could face was learning difficulties. We would see how he developed and if he was okay, he could learn Greek when he was older. It was not the end of the world. The thing was, he overcame each one of his developmental stages quite late. He did not need unnecessary pressure.

When he was about four years old, he would wake up about one o'clock in the morning and come in our room. When my wife questioned him, why he came over, he told her that the angels glided him over. She was and still is a sucker for this kind of talk. The bottom line was; he wanted to get in our bed. My wife would then go in his room, while Petros would get in bed with me. He got away with it for a few months until we put a stop to it. It was cute at first. But enough was enough.

His routine then, was to wake up and ask for a glass of water. The funny thing was that he would not drink water from the tap. It had to be cold. The first few nights I had to go downstairs twice as the second time I had to fill the glass from the fridge. The following week I bought a small fridge and put it on the landing upstairs. It was full of small bottles of water.

Our nightly routine was for Petros to wake up and for me to suddenly see him standing by my side of the bed, asking me to open the bottle. He was half asleep and did not want to be bothered with opening the bottle. He would then very politely say thank you to me and wish me goodnight, on his way to his bed. It never ceased to amaze me how polite he was. He certainly did not take after me, in this respect. It is all down to Vas.

We could always tell when he was about to fall ill. His hearing would drop dramatically and he could hardly hear. Whenever we talked to him, he would come near us and place his ear next to our mouth, indicating to us that he had trouble hearing us. Whenever he did that, the next day he was ill with temperature.

His hearing is just below normal level now. He still needs to wear hearing-aids in both ears and glasses. The hair behind his ear has grown back! The funny thing is, when he goes to answer the phone, he delays because he has to take his hearing aid off so he can hear properly. The hearing aid makes a whistling sound if he does not take it off.

Contrary to earlier predictions, he is just fine. He can speak quite a few Greek words but he says he wants to wake up one morning and be fluent in Greek without doing the hard work. If only the world worked like this!

When my mom calls from Cyprus, and he answers the phone, they will say a few words in Greek, like "Gia sou giagia, isai kala?" "Hello grandmother, are you alright?" My mom will then get excited and forget about his lack of knowledge of the Greek language and she will start asking him questions in Greek. Petros will laugh and pass me the phone, telling me that his grandmother got excited again and started talking as if he was fluent in Greek, which of course he is not. Baby steps. He can learn it at his own pace.

At the beginning when we went to Cyprus the first couple of times, if anyone talked to Petros I obviously had to translate. I still do. The first question was; why hadn't we taught him Greek? You could see the disapproval on their faces. No consideration as to whether he had learning problems or that it could impose extra pressure on him; no consideration that we were lucky to have him…and that not speaking a bloody language was not the end of the world! I tried to avoid those people from then on. They were negative without anything constructive to offer but their ignorance. Our life was richer without them in it. It may sound harsh, but life is hard enough as it is, without having to justify your actions every step of the way. Their view was that, "He looks okay, so he is just like any normal little kid". They were wrong.

Overcoming every aspect of his developmental problems was a constant battle and worry, "I'll be damned if I am going to create extra pressure on him."

One night we wanted to take my parents out for a meal but my dad did not want to go out. He rarely goes out and he prefers to eat at home. In the meantime Petros asked me if we could go to the fair afterwards. I told him that it was up to my dad. If he said, "No" then Petros could not go. So I asked my dad again in Greek, if he wanted to go out for a meal with us and he said no. Petros started crying because he thought my dad said, "No" to him, about going to the fair. He went over to him and with tears in his eyes kept asking him "Why, granddad? Why don't you want me to go the fair, granddad?" Obviously my dad did not understand a word and he thought Petros was upset because he would not come out for dinner with us. He quickly relented. I only told him the truth the day before we left. He was not impressed.

Dealing with Petros' development was challenging but at every step we could see that he was adapting. We could not have reached where we are now without the great help we received from the various hospitals.

Petros is our gift from God.

⁓

I am thankful for having Petros. How I had thought I was going to fall pregnant and how I fell pregnant eventually, are miles apart. Without IVF I don't think I could have fallen pregnant. The three courses of IVF were difficult to deal with. That was a small price to pay, in regards to the reward of eventually having a baby. My pregnancy was extremely difficult. Losing two babies and having one fighting for his life on a minute by minute basis, I found intolerably difficult to deal with at the time. Bringing Petros home and having to deal with the subsequent scares makes you a bit tough, but scars you for life.

Regardless of the above, IVF was successful for us. If I knew what I know now, I would go through it again in a heartbeat. I have nothing but praise for the advances of IVF. I wish every woman that goes through IVF all the best and I hope their journey is smoother than mine. I wish that their babies come to this world healthy and they get to enjoy a normal pregnancy. There is no greater gift than giving birth to your baby!

I would like to thank Mr. Artley; our IVF consultant. We may not support the same football team…but his job has brought fulfillment in our life and to that of countless other families. He now lives in Perth, Australia. He is an IVF consultant for the Concept Fertility Clinic. I hope through his caring nature, he brings as much happiness to the families down under, as he brought to us here in England. God bless you.

I would also like to take this opportunity to thank Queen Elizabeth the Queen Mother Hospital in Margate for taking care of my wife.

I would like to thank Medway Maritime Hospital in Gillingham for looking after my wife and son.

I would like to thank the Queens Hospital in Burton upon Trent for looking after my son.

I would also like to thank the ambulance service. It might not have been your finest hour when you dealt with our case but I am in a position now that I understand and actually support you.

I would also like to thank the nurses and doctors who work tirelessly every day. Whoever I upset from any of the above, you all have my sincere apologies and gratitude. I know that sometimes your work goes unappreciated, but continue on your path of healing and keeping families together. There is no greater vocation that this. Through your work, I am today a husband and a father. At one stage I thought I was going to be neither. God bless you all.

Without the help of the above and God, our life could have gone through a different route; a much worse one. Thank you all.

I don't believe that money determines the richness in your life. You may think it's naïve of me. I believe the richness in life is to have your family around you, healthy and well. Every day, I can't wait to finish work and go home and be with them. This is all the riches in the world I want and it is my legacy.

Also have faith. This is coming from me, when I disowned God, at the first sign of trouble. However, bear with me…Vas prayed at the beginning, to be given the chance of having at least one baby. Even though Vas was carrying two, we ended up with one child. When I was asked about the choice of breathing methods and Petros came second, this resulted in him being treated with the HFOV ventilator. Despite the adversities and gloomy predictions about his future, Petros survived and is doing very well. Vas was knocking on death's door until she had the Holy Communion. It might all have been one big coincidence. I don't think so myself. Did we go through all this agony and torment in order for a non-believer like me to get closer to God? Maybe! I would have liked a more subtle and painless route though. We have been through a terrible ordeal. Vas is the more religious one in our family. She is our beacon. She keeps us together.

Our journey is a journey of pain, despair, devastation and hope. If we had to do it again we would. For now we have Petros; for he has brought us faith and hope.

Petros has grown up to be a polite young person. We are very proud of him and Thank God daily for the gift of him.

The thing I have noticed is when I was feeling helpless the first thing I said was "God, please! Help my family". Generally in our hour of need, His name is the first thing that comes out of our mouths. When things go smoothly he doesn't get a look-in, as we think that life is good, solely because of our own actions.

Life is good at the minute but I have drifted away from God.

Writing this book and remembering what happened has brought to me, an unexpected dose of reality. I remembered! I remembered the pact I made that day I prayed. I remembered how sometimes I was dismissive of my in-laws. I thought that I was the only one in pain. Vas is their flesh and blood. She is their daughter and they have as much right as me to be concerned and worried as I am. Writing this story started with our desire to share our experience. How it ends, is with me remembering my sometimes unreasonable moments and trying to make amends and many apologies.

My in-laws were great. Whenever we needed them, they literally dropped everything and stood by our side. My mom, bless her, is still praying for us as she does not see us often. My dad was worrying in his own way. He is a man of few words. You need to know him to understand him. He is just a bit wary of my translations now.

When you read the brochures about IVF, you will come to a section that says that IVF babies are special because of the extra effort you have to go through in order to realize your dream. Yes it is more dramatic, but the bottom line is; all babies are special irrespective of how they arrive in this world. What makes them special is how well you bring them up. It probably makes the women special for the hoops that they have to go through in order to create their family. For that they have to be supported and congratulated for they are the real heroes of this adventure as well as every other mother on this planet. Mothers, go through the pains of pregnancy and labor. I am sure if men were able to give birth, we would all be a one child family, for we would never have gone through a second pregnancy. Ladies, for that I salute you and thank you!

Remember, if your first IVF does not work, take it on the chin and be depressed by yourself. When you are around your wife or partner be nothing but optimistic; give them lots of cuddles and just be there.

Always think: "If it happened for us, there is a good chance it will happen for you as well."

With all my heart, I wish you the same gift.

In order not to gloss over things, giving you the impression that we came out of this unscathed, I would like to say that I still have my frights when I am at work and I hear the telephone ring. I am quite overprotective of Petros and Vas. Vas has her own demons to deal with, as well. There are certain things she will still not talk about. Well, now we are talking a little bit about it. Baby steps…

Time is a healer and talking about it helps. You never know, reading about it might help you too. Writing about it, seems to have helped me. Vas is not so forthcoming; as she still finds it a bit daunting, reliving that specific time. The only thing I had to do was worry. Vas had to have all those injections, lose every bit of dignity, cesarean, and the terrible ordeal of giving birth and dealing with the after birth nightmares. She has been through a lot and I am not surprised that she is still scarred. This is the reason, I talk more about it. It is a nice world we live in and we must share our experiences, for we can help one another. This is the whole point of this story. It is a story of going through IVF and also about the complications that can arise in any pregnancy, normal or IVF. It is a story of despair and pain but also of faith and hope.

It is a story of celebrating mothers and women who are trying to be mothers, for they are the unsung heroes of humanity. Do not forget them! Buy your wife and mother of your children flowers and say, "Thank you." Buy your mom flowers and say, "Thank you" for bringing you in this world and raising you up. For first timers, like us, buy your wife/partner flowers and say, "Thank you for going through this for us." Tell her that whatever happens, you will always be there for her. Once again I am not being romantic…I just call it as I see it.

Of course we should not forget those lionesses who however much they tried to become mothers, never managed to achieve their dream.

Be there for them. I hope they find fulfillment in other aspects in their lives which will bring the occasional smile on their faces. My heart goes out to you. I hope you find peace and contentment in your lives through other avenues.

Chapter 13

Points About IVF

IVF: Where's all that grief going? theguardian.com. Sep 2013

There may be five million IVF success stories, but for many millions more women, the treatments have failed. So why do we never hear from them?

Explore: grief. Helen James: IVF destroyed my family / Mail Online. dailymail.co.uk. Oct 2010

When my husband and I began our IVF journey in July 2005, I had just turned 36 and my husband 35 (he hadn't been ready to have a family before that and, as luck would have it…

Explore: ivf babies. The pro-lifers adopting 'spare' embryos created… telegraph.co.uk. Oct 2013

For pro-lifers, America's 650000 or so 'spare' embryos—created during IVF and now in cold storage—merit the same rights as any child in need of loving care. Rob Blackhurst talks to...*What is IVF and what are the risks? Live Well: NHS Choices. www.nhs.uk/Livewell/Fertility/Pages/ IVFexplained.aspx. By: NHS Choices, 2011.*

Find out about in vitro fertilisation (IVF), including what it involves, the chances of getting pregnant and the risks of...More articles on: Fertility and conception.

Articles about In Vitro Fertilization: *Chicago Tribune*, articles. chicagotribune.com/keyword/in-vitro-fertilization

In Vitro Fertilization News. Find breaking news, commentary, and archival information about In Vitro Fertilization from the *Chicago Tribune.*

The point of this section is to highlight the risks. My wife had three courses of IVF where the chemicals were injected in her by me. Other unlucky women go through more courses of IVF with still no guarantee of having a baby.

Give these lionesses an in depth analysis of the long term risks to them. It is the least they deserve. In the old days when a woman was giving birth, there was a high risk of her dying. Now with all the medical advances, let's refrain from putting them in danger in a different way. We owe them that much, at least.

IVF is glorious when it works. However, an extremely detailed study should be made, highlighting the risks of defects an IVF baby could have in relation to a baby conceived naturally. Also is there likely to be more birth defects between a fresh embryo and a frozen one? For the professional and busy people who freeze their eggs, with the intention of undergoing IVF at a later stage in their lives, a more informed picture might alter their plans, as far as the timing of the pregnancy is concerned and the method. We are living in the age of information, accessible at a click of a button. This is one study that needs to be brought to the attention of all would be mothers considering the IVF route. It's alright for us men, as our daily life continues uninterrupted apart from our small contribution.

Quite a lot more people choose the IVF route nowadays. You see adverts on the internet of clinics in various countries claiming high success rates of pregnancy if you go to them. The majority of people that go to them are people like us. Desperate to have a child. The thing they see is the high odds they advertise. Once they tried two or three times, money is getting tight. They then start looking at clinics from all over the world which advertise IVF at a fraction of the cost, of what they have to pay back home. Would this result in similar outcomes as botched cosmetic surgeries?

Don't get me wrong. I am not criticizing the IVF process. Far from it. I have nothing but praise for IVF. There is a very thin line between success and failure with this method. It can bring a couple closer together and at the same time, take its toll on them and split them up. A detailed study regarding this will be helpful and insightful. It can actually help couples weather the stormy waters of unsuccessful attempts, if they have at hand this kind of information.

That is why having some sort of idea before you start, might help you to cope better if you are faced with problems. If any of you are faced with similar problems to ours before you throw in the towel, try and remember how loving you were to each other before you started. Try and remember why you started this quest. You wanted to achieve the most noble of dreams; to create life. Be loving, understanding and communicative with each other. You will feel overwhelmed but do not forget your wife is feeling ten times that. Stick it out for her sake as well as yours. I am not the right person to give advice as I got and still get on Vas's nerves. What I know though, is that with the above and faith in God you have a better chance to come out of it intact.

If you are still having problems falling pregnant, there are blogs out there that deal with this. You get to read and talk with other people in the same boat as you. Do not isolate yourself. You are more likely to receive quality support from strangers who are experiencing what you are going through than from a friend or relative who has not got a clue and who will try to give you empty words of encouragement. If you go on the internet and click; blogs on trying to fall pregnant or infertility, you will find lots of blogs with lots of people sharing their experiences as they go along. Follow their story and interact with them.

The other day I was checking some blogs. I clicked on a few of them. How appropriate and to the point. When I started reading it, I felt a chill in my bones. They bare their most intimate stories as they tell their journey and at the same time they are a pillar of support for other women. You may not have the same problems but through these blogs you will find women with similar problems as yours and you can interact with them. It is blogs like this that will help you as well as all the people who participate there; they are all going through what you are going through. When they tell you they understand, you know they do. In my humble opinion, if you are trying to fall pregnant or going through IVF, the less people (friends and family) that know the better.

Epilogue

Three years ago, Petros decided that he wanted to walk to school with his friends. He was driven to and from school every day either by my wife or myself until then. I was not too happy about it, but I relented after a period of four months of continuous badgering by both of them. We would say goodbye to him at the door and he would walk to school, with his friends. I would wait for four minutes and then I would get in my car and follow very slowly behind him. I did that for four days. On the fourth day I was getting strange looks from other parents who were walking their kids to school. Obviously they noticed a suspicious character following the same group of kids every day. I bet they thought I was a pedophile. When I went home and told my wife, she rolled her eyes. She told me that I should not have followed Petros in the first place and unless we let him spread his wings, how was he going to learn about life and cope by himself? I was still worried but I never followed him again. Baby steps! I just worry a lot. I got over him walking to school and now he has already picked out the car that he wants me to buy him when he gets his driving license. I will be a nervous wreck when he is old enough to drive! At least I have a few more years to get used to it.

Vas is more liberal than me. She wants Petros to experience the world and stand on his two feet by himself. I still can't let go. I am probably more scarred than I thought I was. Well, I have to adjust like everything else in life. Vas has brought up Petros to be sensible and well mannered. I am sure he will be alright. I think I am a worrier like my mom. Baby steps!

Petros is fifteen years old, now. He is quite tall for his age. He towers over his mom, which is not very difficult and he is almost as tall as me. Remember, I was worried about his height at the beginning!

Vas is quite strict with him. She does not spoil him, whereas I do. He says that he likes to go shopping with me, as I tend to buy him what he wants. Vas caught on to his trick and gives me a list of the things she refused him. Bless him, he is trying.

With Vas on his case, he will not turn into a spoilt child.

He has got no learning difficulties. The only difficulty he has, is not really wanting to put the work in, to learn Greek and getting up for school in the morning. He claims that school should not start until eleven o'clock. This way he can wake up in his own time. Kids! He has managed to overcome all of his development stages at his own pace. He got there in the end. He still has to wear glasses and hearing aids. Sometimes when I ask him to do something he has selective hearing, claiming he did not hear me. Bless him, he tries! His speech is okay as well. When he is on the Xbox with his mates he will not shut up!

Every few years we receive a request from UKOS to take Petros down to London. They keep a record of the babies who were on the HFOV ventilator and how they progressed in subsequent years. There they perform a barrage of tests on him. By the time they finish, he is out of breath. All is well so far.

Whenever we meet new people we never tell them that Petros is an IVF baby, unless the topic comes up. However, when we meet people who have been trying for a long time to fall pregnant or are in the process of going through IVF, if we are asked to give our opinion, we do so with pleasure. If they want to keep in touch and talk more about it, then that is not a problem.

This club of ours is full of pain, frustration and desperation. When we went through it, we had no one to talk to, but each other. I wished Vas had someone to talk to, who had already gone through this. Following and engaging in a blog like the above would have helped her enormously, instead of only talking to me, when I had and still have no idea about the workings of the female body.

Be there for someone, so they can offload their worries and fears, about what you have already been through. Only someone who has gone through it, can really understand their consuming and unrelenting need, to be a mother. Their desperation every month when they see their period and the daunting worry of going through IVF. Be supportive. Never forget how desperate, helpless and alone you felt. Do not let another would-be mom go through the same experience without being there for her, if you can help it. Be a shoulder for her to cry when she is feeling down or be ready to listen when she wants to vent her frustration. Tell her you understand. Your support will mean more to her than anyone else's. Be a good human being.

Live and help live!

Creating a life, however miniscule your contribution is, is awesome. Bringing your baby home and nurturing him/her and guiding him/her through life, is the best job in the world and the most rewarding. All the pains you have gone through to create that life will eventually be forgotten. Your baby, your joy and your reason for living, will enrich your life beyond your wildest dreams. Ours has and we are thankful.

What you have read here is only a mild version of what is going through in my head. Those eighteen months, were difficult for me. It was relentless torture! The first few years dealing with Petros' development kept me on edge. It was as if I was always waiting with dread for the next scare. I was praying for it not to come but true to its form the next scare came.

For me it did not end there. After all those years I still have horrible nightmares and wake up in a cold sweat. The effect it had on me was overwhelming.

My one wish was to be called mom. This wish was fulfilled through IVF. Through IVF I managed to fall pregnant and give birth to my son. IVF has granted me the most priceless treasure in the world. My treasure calls me mom. I am happy. I hope you get to have your treasure as well and to be called mom. I wish you this, with all my heart. I know it is a hard procedure. I know that it might not work straight away. We had to do it three times before we succeeded. If your first time does not work...be mentally and physically ready before you start the next second time. The same should apply to all subsequent times. My husband was supportive and he was there for me. I hope yours is, as well. You will need understanding and support and you deserve nothing less. Steve got there in the end. We are a happy family.

This is the first time, since the day Petros was born that we can breathe easily, without worrying about his health. This is the first time that we feel comfortable talking about it.

We are a normal family and we are happy. Through IVF, our family is complete.

This is my family:

My wife's name is: **V**aso

My daughter's name is: **A**ndrea

My name is: **S**teve

My son's name is: **P**etros

My son's name is: **X**ristos

We are **V A S P X**

This is Vas and Petros in 2015

Thank you for joining us through our journey of realizing our IVF miracle. Our journey was a rollercoaster. I hope yours is easier. If not, take heart from what we have been through. Have faith and you will hopefully realize your dream as well. You deserve it and with all my heart, I hope you get it.

God Bless you all.

If you enjoyed *All I Ever Wanted Was To Be Called MOM* by Vaspx, you can go on our website www.vaspx.com and subscribe to our newsletter. As a reward for your loyalty you can download free of charge our first in the series of Y/A fantasy series *Realms And The Curse*. Through the newsletter we shall keep you updated about our second book of *All I Ever Wanted Was To Be Called MOM*, where we go into more detail.

Other Books by Vaspx:

Realms And The Curse and *Realms And The Giant's Spear* also by Vaspx and Maninder Singh.

It is also available on Amazon Kindle

Realms And The Curse
myBook.to/REALMS-Curse

Realms And The Giant's Spear
myBook.to/REALMS-Spear

31901059382574

CPSIA information can be obtained at www.ICGtesting.com
Printed in the USA
BVOW05s0920300516

449990BV00004B/101/P

9 781630 476656